MW00974100

University of Georgia
Athens, Georgia

Written by Nicole Gross

Edited by Adam Burns, Meghan Dowdell, and Kevin Nash

Layout by Adam Burns

*Additional contributions by Omid Gohari,
Christina Koshzow, Chris Mason, Joey Rahimi,
and Luke Skurman*

ISBN # 1-4274-0170-5
ISSN # 1552-132x
© Copyright 2006 College Prowler
All Rights Reserved
Printed in the U.S.A.
www.collegeprowler.com

Last Updated 4/10/08

Special Thanks To: Babs Carryer, Andy Hannah, LaunchCyte, Tim O'Brien, Bob Sehlinger, Thomas Emerson, Andrew Skurman, Barbara Skurman, Bert Mann, Dave Lehman, Daniel Fayock, Chris Babyak, The Donald H. Jones Center for Entrepreneurship, Terry Slease, Jerry McGinnis, Bill Ecenberger, Idie McGinty, Kyle Russell, Jacque Zaremba, Larry Winderbaum, Roland Allen, Jon Reider, Team Evankovich, Lauren Varacalli, Abu Noaman, Mark Exler, Daniel Steinmeyer, Jared Cohon, Gabriela Oates, David Koegler, and Glen Meakem.

Bounce-Back Team: Leah Heald, Erica Goss, and Kendra Berberich.

College Prowler®
5001 Baum Blvd.
Suite 750
Pittsburgh, PA 15213

Phone: 1-800-290-2682
Fax: 1-800-772-4972
E-mail: info@collegeprowler.com
Web Site: www.collegeprowler.com

How this all started...

When I was trying to find the perfect college, I used every resource that was available to me. I went online to visit school websites; I talked with my high school guidance counselor; I read book after book; I hired a private counselor. Sure, this was all very helpful, but nothing really told me what life was like at the schools I cared about. These sources weren't giving me enough information to be totally confident in my decision.

In all my research, there were only two ways to get the information I wanted.

The first was to physically visit the campuses and see if things were really how the brochures described them, but this was quite expensive and not always feasible. The second involved a missing ingredient: the students. Actually talking to a few students at those schools gave me a taste of the information that I needed so badly. The problem was that I wanted more but didn't have access to enough people.

In the end, I weighed my options and decided on a school that felt right and had a great academic reputation, but truth be told, the choice was still very much a crapshoot. I had done as much research as any other student, but was I 100 percent positive that I had picked the school of my dreams?

Absolutely not.

My dream in creating *College Prowler* was to build a resource that people can use with confidence. My own college search experience taught me the importance of gaining true insider insight; that's why the majority of this guide is composed of quotes from actual students. After all, shouldn't you hear about a school from the people who know it best?

I hope you enjoy reading this book as much as I've enjoyed putting it together. Tell me what you think when you get a chance. I'd love to hear your college selection stories.

Luke Skurman
CEO and Co-Founder
lukeskurman@collegeprowler.com

Welcome to College Prowler®

During the writing of College Prowler's guidebooks, we felt it was critical that our content was unbiased and unaffiliated with any college or university. We think it's important that our readers get honest information and a realistic impression of the student opinions on any campus—that's why if any aspect of a particular school is terrible, we (unlike a campus brochure) intend to publish it. While we do keep an eye out for the occasional extremist—the cheerleader or the cynic—we take pride in letting the students tell it like it is. We strive to create a book that's as representative as possible of each particular campus. Our books cover both the good and the bad, and whether the survey responses point to recurring trends or a variation in opinion, these sentiments are directly and proportionally expressed through our guides.

College Prowler guidebooks are in the hands of students throughout the entire process of their creation. Because you can't make student-written guides without the students, we have students at each campus who help write, randomly survey their peers, edit, layout, and perform accuracy checks on every book that we publish. From the very beginning, student writers gather the most up-to-date stats, facts, and inside information on their colleges. They fill each section with student quotes and summarize the findings in editorial reviews. In addition, each school receives a collection of letter grades (A through F) that reflect student opinion and help to represent contentment, prominence, or satisfaction for each of our 20 specific categories. Just as in grade school, the higher the mark the more content, more prominent, or more satisfied the students are with the particular category.

Once a book is written, additional students serve as editors and check for accuracy even more extensively. Our bounce-back team—a group of randomly selected students who have no involvement with the project—are asked to read over the material in order to help ensure that the book accurately expresses every aspect of the university and its students. This same process is applied to the 200-plus schools College Prowler currently covers. Each book is the result of endless student contributions, hundreds of pages of research and writing, and countless hours of hard work. All of this has led to the creation of a student information network that stretches across the nation to every school that we cover. It's no easy accomplishment, but it's the reason that our guides are such a great resource.

When reading our books and looking at our grades, keep in mind that every college is different and that the students who make up each school are not uniform—as a result, it is important to assess schools on a case-by-case basis. Because it's impossible to summarize an entire school with a single number or description, each book provides a dialogue, not a decision, that's made up of 20 different topics and hundreds of student quotes. In the end, we hope that this guide will serve as a valuable tool in your college selection process. Enjoy!

OMID GOHARI ◯ CHRISTINA KOSHZOW ◯ CHRIS MASON ◯ JOEY RAHIMI ◯ LUKE SKURMAN ◯
The College Prowler Team

UNIVERSITY OF GEORGIA

Table of Contents

Introduction from the Author

If you had told me in high school that I would end up at the University of Georgia, I would have told you to lay off the crack pipe. Initially, I did not want to come to UGA. I had this preconceived notion of what college would be like, and what kind of people I would meet, and at first, I did not think UGA fit in this vision. Well, as It turned out, I was 150 percent wrong.

I ended up coming to UGA for two reasons: everyone I knew there seemed to be having a blast; and the HOPE scholarship paid for my tuition, so I could basically go there for free. I was not one of those kids who came in knowing bundles of people already enrolled there. I am the oldest child in my family, and from Valdosta, GA, where only a handful of high school seniors choose to go to UGA each year. I started college life almost entirely from scratch, which was extremely daunting in the beginning, because, let's be honest, UGA is a big school. I didn't have a major, I didn't know a single girl on my hall, I didn't know which bus to take, and the list of the other things I didn't know went on for about six miles. But if you can make it through the first month—aiming to talk to at least one new person each day—I promise that, by the end of your freshman year, the effort will be well worth it.

The fact that I am entering my senior year now is overwhelmingly sad, because while I wasn't paying attention to it, I have carved out exactly the kind of college life I always wanted to have. When I graduate and am not able to live this kind of life anymore, I'm pretty sure I'll miss it every single day. I have seen plays, protests, concerts, and other heralding events that I know I'll never forget. I have seen my friends perform really bad karaoke, and I have even seen a camel chewing on grass on the campus quad. I have been to football games, basketball games, gymnastics meets, fashion shows, a dozen different bars, festivals of beer, bike races, tailgates, and all these things I experienced even before I left to go home following freshman year.

I wanted to write this book to let you know exactly what goes on in Athens, and what you should expect to gain from college life at UGA. I don't know if these are going to be the best years of my life yet, but I wouldn't be surprised if they were. If this sounds like a school you can picture yourself at, then you can consider this your lucky day, because you've just stumbled upon the biggest and best "cheat sheet" out there.

Nicole Goss, Author
University of Georgia

By the Numbers

General Information

The University of Georgia
212 Terrell Hall
Athens, GA 30602

Control:
Public

Academic Calendar:
Semester

Religious Affiliation:
None

Founded:
January 27, 1785

Web Site:
www.uga.edu

Main Phone:
(706) 542-3000

Student Body

**Full-Time
Undergraduates:**
23,418

**Part-Time
Undergraduates:**
1,917

**Total Male
Undergraduates:**
10,742

**Total Female
Undergraduates:**
14,593

Admissions

Overall Acceptance Rate:
55%

Early Decision Acceptance Rate:
Not offered

Early Action Acceptance Rate:
N/A

Regular Acceptance Rate:
55%

Total Applicants:
16,871

Total Acceptances:
9,242

Freshman Enrollment:
4,721

Yield (% of admitted students who actually enroll):
51%

Early Action Deadline:
October 15

Early Action Notification:
December 15

Regular Decision Deadline:
January 15

Regular Decision Notification:
Rolling starting December 15

Must-Reply-By Date:
May 1

Applicants Placed on Waiting List:
502

Applicants Accepting a Place on Waiting List:
342

Students Enrolled from Waiting List:
175

Transfer Applications Received:
2,654

Transfer Applicants Accepted:
1,524

Transfer Students Enrolled:
1,133

Transfer Application Acceptance Rate:
57%

Common Application Accepted?
No

SAT I or ACT Required?
Either

SAT I Range (25th–75th Percentile):
1130–1310

SAT I Verbal Range (25th–75th Percentile):
560–660

SAT I Math Range (25th–75th Percentile):
570–650

ACT Composite Range (25th–75th Percentile):
25–29

ACT English Range (25th–75th Percentile):
25–31

ACT Math Range (25th–75th Percentile):
24–29

Freshman Retention Rate:
93%

Top 10% of High School Class:
50%

Application Fee:
$50

Online Application:
www.admissions.uga.edu/ apply_now.html

Admissions Phone:
(706) 542-8776

Admissions E-Mail:
undergrad@admissions. uga.edu

Admissions Web Site:
www.admissions.uga.edu

Financial Information

Full-Time Tuition:
$4,159 in-state
$18,128 out-of-state   .

Room and Board:
$7,292

Books and Supplies:
$840

Average Need-Based Financial Aid Package (including loans, work-study, grants, and other sources):
$8,170

Students Who Applied For Financial Aid:
46%

Applicants Who Received Aid:
58%

Financial Aid Forms Deadline:
March 1

Financial Aid Phone:
(706) 542-6147

Financial Aid E-mail:
osfa@uga.edu

Financial Aid Web Site:
www.uga.edu/osfa

Academics

The Lowdown On...
Academics

Degrees Awarded:
Bachelor's
Post-bachelor's certificate
Master's
Post-master's certificate
Doctorate
First professional

Most Popular Majors:
20.3% Business/marketing
10.3% Social sciences
 9.1% Education
 8.2% Biological/life sciences
 6.1% Psychology

Full-Time Faculty:
1,733

Faculty with Terminal Degree:
94%

Student-to-Faculty Ratio:
18:1

Average Course Load:
15 hours

Undergraduate Schools:

College of Agricultural and Environmental Sciences

College of Education

College of Environment and Design

College of Family and Consumer Sciences

College of Pharmacy

College of Public Health

College of Veterinary Medicine

Franklin College of Arts and Sciences

Grady College of Journalism and Mass Communication

Odum School of Ecology

School of Law

(Schools, continued)

School of Public and International Affairs

School of Social Work

Terry College of Business

Warnell School of Forestry and Natural Resources

Class Sizes:

Fewer than 20 Students: 38%

20 to 49 Students: 50%

50 or More Students: 11%

Graduation Rates:

Four-Year: 48%

Five-Year: 74%

Six-Year: 78%

Special Degree Options

Accelerated program, cooperative education program, cross-registration, distance learning, double major, dual enrollment, exchange student program (domestic), external degree program, honors program, independent study, internships, liberal arts/career combination, student-designed major, study abroad, teacher certification program

Pre-professional programs: Forest resources, journalism, landscape architecture, medical technology, nursing, pre-dentistry, pre-law, pre-medicine, pre-optometry, pre-veterinary science, pre-pharmacy, pre-theology

Combined-degree programs: Five-year landscape architecture program, bachelor's/master's degree honors programs, dentistry program with Medical College of Georgia

Cooperative education programs: Agriculture, art, business, computer science, education, engineering, health professions, home economics, humanities, natural science, social/behavioral science, technologies, vocational arts

AP Test Score Requirements

Acceptable scores vary depending on the major.

IB Test Score Requirements

Acceptable scores vary depending on the major.

Best Places to Study

Law Library, Main Library, North Campus under a tree, Science Library, Starbucks, Student Learning Center

Sample Academic Clubs

American Association of Textile Chemists and Colorists, American Society of Agricultural Engineers, Demosthenian Society, National Association of Black Journalists, Phi Kappa Literary Society, *Red and Black* newspaper, The UGA Block and Bridle Club

Did You Know?

UGA is rated to be more selective in accepting applications than many state schools because there is such **a high turnover rate** in converting those accepted into those that actually enroll.

Students Speak Out On...
Academics

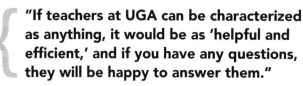

"If teachers at UGA can be characterized as anything, it would be as 'helpful and efficient,' and if you have any questions, they will be happy to answer them."

Q "I was in the business school, and I feel that **I had the best teachers on campus**."

Q "I have had some wonderful teachers, and even though **you will have some large classes your freshman year**, your teachers will have office hours, and will be very willing to provide help."

Q "I found that there was **a general apathy regarding many classes**, which I thought I left behind in high school. Since I am motivated (mostly) to perform well academically, I hated this aspect of UGA."

Q "All of **your first-year classes will have over 300 people in them**. It isn't that bad. You get to sleep if want to, and check out all the hot girls or guys."

Q "I feel like I am getting a really good education at Georgia. I know people who have graduated from here, and they were able to get **really excellent jobs within a few years after graduation**."

Q "It would be a lie to say that all the teachers here are interesting, but **there are definitely those teachers that clearly love the material** and love teaching."

Q "Most of **the professors I have had are very eccentric**, and more lively than my high school teachers. I find my professors to hold a broad knowledge of their material and present it with enthusiasm and a blend of personal background."

Q "Since most of my classes are huge lecture classes, **I didn't really get to know any of the teachers** personally, but I think at the very least, all of my teachers have been very fair in their policies. In all the office hours I have been to, they have been extremely willing to help in any way. As for the classes, some are interesting, while others you just have to take to graduate. I think the interest factor mostly depends on the teacher anyway."

Q "The teachers I have had here are a mixed bag. I've had some very interesting ones and some who made class last forever. It really **all depends on the subject** you're learning, and whether they can make you excited about the topic."

Q "The **core classes can be really, really boring** because you're probably not at all interested in the material and are only taking the classes to fill a certain requirement. Once you get into your major, the classes are really interesting, and the professors will really try to help you with work and internship stuff."

Q "If a student takes the time to get to know their teacher, the teacher makes the effort to get to know the student. I have had teachers that have genuinely taken the time to help out when needed. Several of my teachers have made the content of their courses apply to my life and interests. **There are lecture classes, as well as small intimate classes available for students**."

Q "Some of my teachers have been truly horrible, but others have been okay. I haven't had any that blew me away or anything, but for the most part, **they were pretty darn helpful**."

The College Prowler Take On...
Academics

Oftentimes, UGA attracts both students who want to learn and students who want to party. UGA has a dubious reputation for being a "party school," but make no mistake about it, you will not be able to slack on your studies and leave here four years later with a diploma. Don't get me wrong, having fun is an extremely important part of the college experience, but eventually, you have to put in the study time, or you won't make it through sophomore year. Some classes, particularly freshman classes, are very big, easily filling auditoriums that hold a couple hundred, but the professors really try to make themselves accessible, for the most part. Professors always encourage students to stop by their offices for help or for study reviews. Most large classes will break down into discussion groups once a week with a teaching assistant (TA), who is usually a recent graduate student from a local school. The TAs are usually a little stressed out and/or overwhelmed, but in the end, they prove to be very helpful and relate extremely well with the students in their breakout groups. It is, however, not uncommon to have teachers—at any level—that speak little to no English, and this is obviously a problem.

There are a plethora of majors at UGA. Some of the more atypical ones include agricultural business operations, landscaping, and plant pathology; I have never once heard someone complain that UGA doesn't offer a major they want.

The College Prowler® Grade on

Academics: B

A high Academics grade generally indicates that professors are knowledgeable, accessible, and genuinely interested in their students' welfare. Other determining factors include class size, how well professors communicate, and whether or not classes are engaging.

Local Atmosphere

The Lowdown On...
Local Atmosphere

Region:
South

City, State:
Athens, GA

Setting:
College town

Distance from Atlanta:
1 hour

Points of Interest:
The Arch
Downtown Athens
Georgia State Botanical Gardens

Closest Shopping Malls or Plazas:
Georgia Square Mall
Mall of Georgia

→

Closest Movie Theaters:

Beechwood Cinema
Beechwood Plaza
(706) 546-1011

Carmike 12
1575 Lexington Rd.
(706) 354-0016

(Movie Theaters, continued)
Georgia Square Cinemas
(movies for $1)
3700 Atlanta Highway
(706) 548-3023

City Web Sites:

www.uga.edu/uga/Athens.html
www.visitathensga.com

Did You Know?

5 Fun Facts about Athens:

1. John Mayer's "No Such Thing" video was **filmed in downtown Athens** at the Georgia Theater.

2. *Road Trip*, starring **Tom Green and Breckin Myer**, was filmed in Athens around UGA.

3. Ben Affleck bought a house in Athens, GA. He supposedly eats at **Five and Ten** in Five Points when in town.

4. The **Athens Transit public transportation bus** is actually called The Bus.

5. **On game days**, Athens becomes one of the largest cities in Georgia. Sell-out crowds guarantee over 92,000 people will be in Athens.

Famous People from Athens:

Michael Stipe, and Katie from MTV's *Surf Girls*

Local Slang:

BrewFest – An annual tasting of national brand beers
Coke – Any kind of carbonated beverage
Twilight – A bike race every spring that runs through downtown

Students Speak Out On...
Local Atmosphere

{ **"Athens is definitely a college town. It's called the 'Classic City,' and it fits that name very well. I love Athens, and I never want to leave. I miss Athens when I go home—even just for spring break."**

Q "**Athens is what I had always imagined a college town would be like**. The school's campus is gorgeous, and UGA is located in a large town that revolves around the University. There are tons of thing to do, and you are only an hour and a half away from Atlanta, which is a great city. You will meet lots people from Atlanta, and chances are, your roommate will be from Atlanta and you will have the opportunity to go home with him or her for a weekend or two."

Q "Downtown Athens is the place to be! There are theaters, restaurants, clubs, bars, and street performers, all of which are very cheap. You can't beat it. Athens is a great town to be young and energetic, because **there is so much to do there**. The weekend before I left Athens to come back home for the summer, I went to a carnival, saw a movie at a drive-in, went bar hopping, kayaking, to a concert, and played basketball."

Q "**This city definitely has a college-like atmosphere**. Students comprise most of the city's population, and most of the local businesses thrive on students' commerce. Truett-McConnell is kind of like a community college and is close to UGA. We also have Athens Tech, but most of the student population comes from UGA."

Q "**Athens has a great, small, Southern-town feel**! The town itself is beautiful. It's very historic and has lots of character. Visit the Arch when you come down here—it's the University's trademark."

Q "**The atmosphere in this town is amazing**—I love it here; it's a quintessential college town. There is always something for students to do, whether it be shopping, eating, concerts, or going out."

Q "The only time I have ever been bored in Athens was when I was here over the summer taking classes. Once classes begin in the fall, **there is honestly something going on every single day**, whether it's a concert, a game, or just a group of people sitting by the pool."

Q "The atmosphere constantly reminds students that they are in a college town. While it is a residential town, as well, students make up the most abundant population here. Overall, **the community and the University work well together**. Athens Tech is very close by as well."

Q "**I love living in Athens** because there always seems to be something for people my age to do. Where I'm from, it's usually so boring. Since I've lived here, though, I have rarely been bored."

Q "Athens is a small town when you take out the student population, and if you're here **over the summer it can be really boring**, but once the students get back in the fall, there's lots to do—definitely more than any other small town in Georgia."

Q "**There is almost too much to do in Athens**. I have had to call home to ask for money many times because I go out and do so many things."

Q "If I had to guess, I would say local Athenians probably get **tired of seeing college kids all the time**."

The College Prowler Take On...
Local Atmosphere

Athens, the 'Classic City,' is the quintessential college town. Downtown offers amazing nightlife, with numerous clubs, bars, cafés, restaurants, and shops on every corner. Music is a cornerstone of downtown Athens, with plenty of opportunities for students to see local and nationally-famous bands. REM, the B-52s, and Widespread Panic all got their start in Athens. Students agree that bars are the place to be. They're always packed from Thursday night to the wee hours of Sunday morning. Unlike some towns, Athens actually has enough bars to accommodate the number of partygoers living here. There are freshman bars that are a little less selective as far as fake IDs go, as well as sports bars, outdoor bars, and sophisticated, ritzy bars. Downtown is located within walking distance from the dorms, so walking to and from parties is not a problem, and nobody has to drive. Taxis and student-sponsored organizations also provide transportation to and from various hotspots.

The Classic Center brings a little art and culture to Athens. The Classic Center has hosted a performance of *RENT*, a night with Lauryn Hill, stand-up comedy with John Leguizamo, and the *Nutcracker* ballet. Each and every student at UGA can be a part of something, if they so choose. And if you get tired of being in a smaller town, Atlanta is about an hour away. Anything Athens doesn't have, Atlanta definitely does.

A-

The College Prowler® Grade on

Local Atmosphere: A-

A high Local Atmosphere grade indicates that the area surrounding campus is safe and scenic. Other factors include nearby attractions, proximity to other schools, and the town's attitude toward students.

Safety & Security

The Lowdown On...
Safety & Security

Number of UGA Police:
71

UGA Police Phone:
Emergencies: (706) 542-2200
Other calls: (706) 542-0097
TTY: (706) 542-1188

Safety Services:
Emergency phones
Escort services
Hand-scanning identification system in dorms
Self-defense classes
Watchdawgs

Health Services:

The University Health Center offers basic medical services, an on-site pharmacy, STD screening, HIV testing, counseling, nutrition classes, and psychological services.

Health Center:

(706) 542-1162

Hours: Fall and Spring Semesters: Monday–Friday 8 a.m.–8 p.m., Saturday–Sunday 10 a.m.–5 p.m.; Summer: Monday–Friday 8 a.m.–5 p.m., Saturday 9 a.m.–12 p.m.

Did You Know?

There are **25 call-boxes** sprinkled throughout the UGA campus.

All **UGA police officers are college educated** and many attend graduate programs.

The Patrol Division is organized into three patrol shifts, which **operate 24 hours a day**, 365 days a year.

Each patrol shift is assigned one lieutenant, one sergeant, two corporals, and numerous patrol officers to **effectively safeguard the University community and the surrounding area**.

Students Speak Out On...
Safety & Security

"The campus seems pretty secure. I've never really felt unsafe on campus. It is a little eerie at night, but that's the way things always are. All in all, I would say it's very safe here."

Q "The **campus is an overall safe place**. Obviously, common sense is a critical virtue to possess in a campus environment that includes over 30,000 different people. Some of the services that the University provides are emergency call-boxes, hand-scan stations for entering dorms, and an organization called Watchdawgs that provides students with free rides home from downtown after a night at the bars. Overall, UGA provides a safe environment for all."

Q "I wouldn't suggest walking alone at night in Athens. **There have been a few rapes** of girls who were drunk and walking home alone on campus at night. Don't do that! That's the same thing that would happen anywhere, you know?"

Q "Security is pretty good. **I've always felt very safe on campus**, **even at night** walking to and from my car at the library. When I lived in the dorms my freshman year, I felt very safe at all times."

Q "Security on campus has been quite a problem for the past few years. There have been several rapes, and a number of attacks on students. However, most of these attacks could have been avoided. **Having some street smarts would prevent a lot of those incidents**."

Q "I've never felt in any kind of danger on campus. There are some dorms located across the street from housing projects, but I lived there, and I never once had a problem with anything. **Sometimes cars parked along that street get broken into during the day**, though."

Q "Most areas are sufficiently lit, and **campus police frequently circulate the campus**."

Q "I heard a story one time about a girl that got raped walking home from downtown, but other than that, I don't remember any other scary stories. **I have not experienced any kind of danger** myself."

Q "**I wouldn't park in the 'rape lot' after dark**, but I honestly don't really feel in danger when I'm on campus."

Q "**You can see the campus police driving around** all day long, just kind of looking out for anything suspicious. So, I usually feel very safe."

Q "The worst things I've ever heard of happening while I've been here, were that a couple of cars got broken into on Baxter Street. **I don't like walking alone at night**, but other than that, I feel pretty much safe all the time."

Q "The only time I ever felt unsafe was when **there were bomb threats called in**. They had to clear out some buildings, and the buses stopped running and everything. That was kind of scary, but I think they got it under control pretty fast."

The College Prowler Take On...
Safety & Security

Overall, UGA students feel safe on campus about 99 percent of the time. Walking home from downtown can potentially be dangerous, especially if you are alone—some people have been mugged and even raped doing so. Students should always travel in groups. The downtown cops are mainly there to bust underage drinkers, and they are usually out in droves, so trying to run from them doesn't always work. There are campus police everywhere you look, as well as Athens-Clarke County cops. There are call-boxes all over the place, too. The streets and parking lots are well lit, but some of the parking structures are in shady areas that are not the greatest places to be at night. Security at major events has increased year after year since 9/11, so fans can expect their purses and cargo pant pockets to be searched at the entrance to every football game and at most other sporting events. There are also cops at the gate who run metal-detector tests on random or suspicious fans. There are plenty of security officials and cops around on game days, so incidents are kept to a minimum. Also, on game days, cops are pretty lax on enforcing drinking laws, allowing open containers and drunk minors to slide by without being bothered.

In terms of health services, the University Health Center is usually a little crowded, but there are good doctors available, and the pharmacy is located in the same building. There are also alcohol awareness classes at the Health Center for those unlucky students who were caught drinking underage in the dorms.

B-

The College Prowler® Grade on

Safety & Security: B-

A high grade in Safety & Security means that students generally feel safe, campus police are visible, blue-light phones and escort services are readily available, and safety precautions are not overly necessary.

Computers

The Lowdown On...
Computers

High-Speed Network?
Yes

Wireless Network?
Yes

Number of Labs:
9

Number of Computers:
849

Operating Systems:
PC, Mac, and UNIX

24-Hour Labs:
Yes

Charge to Print?
Yes, usually around six or seven cents per page

Free Software

Adobe Acrobat Reader 5.0, Accessibility Software, Adobe
Photoshop, Arches on the Web, Chemistry Resources,
F Secure Anti-Virus, Internet Explorer 6, Maple 7, Math Tutorial
Software, Microsoft Excel XP, Microsoft Office, Microsoft Photo
Editor, Microsoft Powerpoint XP, Microsoft Word XP, OASIS
on the Web, SSH Secure Shell Client and TN3270, Stuffit
Expander, Windows 2000, WS-FTP

Did You Know?

The Student Learning Center houses 500
computers and has **1,000 Internet ports** for
students with laptops.

Beautiful Herty Field on North Campus offers
wireless Internet access to students, and can
accommodate 30 to 60 simultaneous connections.

Students Speak Out On...
Computers

{ **"There are computers available everywhere! If one lab happens to be crowded, another is just around the corner. Also, the University's network is easy to access anywhere."**

Q "It is not mandatory that you bring your own computer, but it helps. Most dorms have a computer lab located on site, and there are many other computer lab locations all around campus. Some of the labs do get crowded at peak times (around noon most days and also on days when large classes have projects to turn in). **Every dorm has access to cable modems in its rooms**, and the network is pretty reliable."

Q "Only during class registration times are computer labs pretty crowded. You can almost always find an empty computer at one of the many computer labs. If you can **bring your own computer, it might make things easier** on you, but going to the lab can be beneficial because you'll finish what you need to finish. The only bad thing about the labs is that they aren't open 24/7. They each have different operating hours depending on the day of the week."

Q "The computer labs are not as big as some might like them to be. **The labs are usually empty**, except during registration periods at the beginning of each semester. As someone who has a vast knowledge of computers, I would highly recommend bringing your own."

Q "The computer network is different for each dorm. I lived in Russell Hall, which I think is the most fun dorm at UGA. We had an Ethernet connection, but sometimes it was kind of slow because they had just installed it and were still trying to fix all of the glitches. The computer labs are usually not crowded because **most people bring their own computer**. I recommend that you bring your own computer because it will make life much easier on you."

Q "On campus, **the computers tend to be pretty fast, but lack certain programs**. I don't normally use the computer labs, except when I am in the library between classes. The computers tend to be occupied, but there is never a long wait for a computer. Since many classes are on WebCT, I think having your own personal computer is vital and convenient."

Q "**The computer network in my dorm was amazing** because it was brand new, and I could download anything at great speeds, but I was also in a smaller dorm. Sophomore year, I used the Terry undergrad computer lab a lot, and it was usually crowded, but I always found a seat. I would definitely recommend bringing your own computer; it's not a necessity, but it is more convenient. However, I use my computer more for AIM and downloading songs than anything else."

Q "The computer network is great here. **There are computers everywhere**. Although not extremely convenient, you could easily come here without a computer and survive four years. The Student Learning Center has a ton of computers and is a great place to use one."

Q "I brought my own computer, and I don't know what I would do if I didn't have one in my room, because I am obsessed with instant messaging, and I check my e-mail probably five times a day. But, **plenty of people just use the ones in the dorm labs** and at the SLC."

Q "The **computers at the SLC are fast**, so any time I have something complicated to do, I like to go there. They are much faster than my computer, which even has DSL. There are also scanners, and some software on the SLC computers that you may not have on your own computer."

Q "**I would die without my own computer**, but plenty of people don't mind doing all their stuff in the labs, or at the SLC."

Q "Our **Internet connection in the dorms is down all the time, and it's really frustrating**. I'll be in the middle of a timed quiz, and it will cut off, and I'll be screwed. Getting help with stuff like that has also been a huge pain because the EITS people are so hard to get in touch with."

The College Prowler Take On...
Computers

At UGA you've got dorm labs, the computers in the libraries, and the computers in the Student Learning Center (SLC) at your disposal. The computers in the SLC are new and extremely fast. Some of them have Instant Messenger already downloaded on them, so you can chat between classes if you like. It's a hassle to print anything because you have to charge it to your UGA ID, and in order to do that, you must have available funds on your card. To put money on your card, you have to go to a "money-card conversion machine." There are a few in the main library, one in the Tate Student Center, and a few in the Student Learning Center. The computers in the dorms have Ethernet service, which is usually great, but sometimes the entire system crashes, and everyone is forced to go without Internet access for hours, and sometimes days!

On registration days, it can be difficult to find a free computer in the libraries or at the SLC. Sometimes, you have to wait for one to free up. The Student Learning Center has 500 new computers, and 1,000 data ports, which alleviated a lot of the congestion in the library computer labs.

The College Prowler® Grade on

Computers: B

A high grade in Computers designates that computer labs are available, the computer network is easily accessible, and the campus' computing technology is up-to-date.

Facilities

The Lowdown On...
Facilities

Student Center:
The Tate Student Center

Athletic Center:
The Ramsey Center

Libraries:
4

Campus Size:
614 acres

Popular Places to Chill:
Blue Sky Coffee (downtown)
North Campus
Ramsey Center
Starbucks (downtown)
Student Learning Center
Tate Center

What Is There to Do on Campus?

There are often demonstrations around central campus or information fairs for students at the Tate Student Center. The Tate Center has plenty of seating for reading, studying, or talking with friends. There is also a game room with ping pong, pool, and arcade games. The Bulldog Café adjacent to Tate offers many options for lunch, and the new Student Learning Center has a coffeehouse with outdoor seating. North Campus is a very popular area for students to relax, read, or have a picnic.

Movie Theater on Campus?

Yes, there is a movie theater in the Tate Center.

Bar on Campus?

No

Bowling on Campus?

No, but downtown is right across the street from North Campus.

Coffeehouse on Campus?

Yes, Jittery Joe's in the Student Learning Center.

Favorite Things to Do

Meet friends for lunch at Bulldog Café or hang out at the Student Learning Center (the place to see and be seen), play ultimate Frisbee on the Myers quad, nap on North Campus, head downtown for lunch or a coffee, work out at Ramsey Center.

Did You Know?

Soccer, volleyball and rhythmic gymnastics events for the 1996 Centennial Olympic Games in Atlanta **were held in UGA's** Stegeman Coliseum and Sanford Stadium.

Students Speak Out On...
Facilities

> **"The facilities on campus are great. The Ramsey Center, where students exercise, is amazing. The Tate Center is a good place to hang out and is a good meeting place."**

Q "**The athletic facilities are impressive** and probably the most impressive aspect of campus. We have an $83 million student fitness center that houses an indoor track, indoor olympic-size pool complete with diving, numerous dance and aerobic studios, eight basketball courts, a gymnastics area, two volleyball courts, and two separate weight-training facilities."

Q "Our student center has a **movie theater that runs new movies, classic movies, and sneak previews** of upcoming movies (I saw *Road Trip* two months before it came out in theaters), as well as the Bulldog Café, study rooms, art galleries, the bookstore, and it's the hub for advertisements and offices that can help get you involved in the thousands of activities that take place at UGA."

Q "The facilities here are wonderful. The Ramsey Center, which houses the gym, is the place where many athletes go to train. **It is considered one of the top three gymnasiums of any university** in the country. If you like to work out, you'll be in heaven here."

Q "**The Student Learning Center (SLC) and the Ramsey Center are probably the most popular places** on campus, and they are always filled with students because they're good places to get work done or work out, as well as good places to meet people and hang out. The SLC is also really nice, with a coffee shop that is conducive to hanging out."

Q "The workout center is endless, with available equipment and venues to meet everyone's interests. You name it, it's there—from swimming to racquetball, weight lifting to Pilates classes. There is **a new student center equipped with Internet access** where many students go to study individually, as well as in groups. There are designated quiet areas, but also rooms that are appropriate for discussions. Students love it!"

Q "I think **the new Student Learning Center is a beautiful building and very functional**. I love to go there to study and hang out, and the coffee shop was a great idea."

Q "I sometimes go swimming in the lap pools at the Ramsey Center, and those are in pretty good shape. Ramsey in general is pretty nice, especially the courts, and **the rock-climbing wall is pretty cool**."

Q "Some of **the classrooms are really old**, and the ones in Park Hall, for example, smell like a sweaty gym. The new rooms in the SLC are really nice, though, and have comfy chairs with lots of leg room."

Q "**I think the facilities are pretty good** considering how big the school is. The places people go most, like the Tate Center, the SLC, and the Ramsey area probably are the best."

Q "The **SLC is probably the nicest building** I've ever been in on campus. There are marble steps, leather chairs, and a really nice library. I was actually pretty impressed by it all."

The College Prowler Take On...
Facilities

UGA's facilities are impressive, to say the least. The Student Learning Center (SLC) is a major asset to the campus. Aside from computers, the SLC boasts 26 new state-of-the-art classrooms, 96 private-group study rooms with marker boards, and wireless Internet access. The interior of the SLC is surprisingly elegant, and during finals week, the SLC is the place to be for many students—it is open 24 hours and is generally packed the whole time. The libraries are extremely large, with many areas to study. The main library also offers a few small theaters, where students watch cultural films and newer movies, as well as lounges where students can talk louder than in normal study areas.

The Tate Center is centrally located and always surrounded by activity. Many Dawgs After Dark events are held there, as it houses a movie theater, game room, and several other venues. Ramsey is also very popular with students. There are aerobic rooms, gymnastics facilities, pools, a rock-climbing wall, state-of-the-art workout equipment, and badminton, basketball, racquetball, and volleyball courts and at every turn. You can even sign up for a personal trainer. Aerobics classes fill up fast, and there is often a wait for an elliptical machine no matter when you go. For its impressive size, Ramsey has a surprisingly small number of machines in the gym area. However, *Sports Illustrated* ranked Ramsey as the best college fitness facility in the nation in 2004, and students flock to it. In general, facilities are good, but some buildings are in need of renovation, including many of the science facilities and some dorms.

The College Prowler® Grade on
Facilities: A-

A high Facilities grade indicates that the campus is aesthetically pleasing and well-maintained; facilities are state-of-the-art, and libraries are exceptional. Other determining factors include the quality of both athletic and student centers and an abundance of things to do on campus.

Campus Dining

The Lowdown On...
Campus Dining

Freshman Meal Plan Requirement?

No

Meal Plan Cost:

$2,192 for 5-day plan
$2,394 for 7-day plan

Places to Grab a Bite with Your Meal Plan:

Bolton Dining Commons

Food: Cereal station, deli sandwiches, home-style buffets, ice cream and dessert bars, "smart" options, salad bar, soups

Location: Baxter Street, near high-rise dorms

Hours: Daily 7 a.m.–7 p.m.

➡

Oglethorpe Dining Commons

Food: Cereal station, 24-item dessert bar, french fries, grilled chicken sandwiches, hamburgers, home-style buffet, ice cream, premium entrées on Saturday nights, salad bar, Sunday brunch

Location: Off Lumpkin Street, next to Oglethorpe House

Hours: Monday–Friday
7 a.m.–7 p.m.,
Saturday 8:30 a.m.–7 p.m.,
Sunday 8:30 a.m.–2 p.m.

Snelling Dining Hall

Food: Cereal station, dessert bar, French fries, Giorgio's Pizza, hamburgers, home-style buffets, hot sandwiches and cheesesteaks, pasta, salad bar

Location: South Campus

Hours: Monday–Thursday
7 a.m.–12 a.m.,
Friday 7 a.m.–2:30 p.m.

The Village Summit

Food: Focuses on made-to-order items, such as omelets from Egg Works, pizza from Giorgio & Co., and sandwiches at Blue Steel Grill and Upper East Side

Location: East Village Commons

Hours: Monday–Friday
7 a.m.–8 p.m.,
Saturday 8:30 a.m.–8 p.m.,
Sunday 8:30 a.m.–2 p.m.

24-Hour On-Campus Eating?

No

Student Favorite

Snelling Dining Hall

Other Options

The Student Learning Center houses a Jittery Joe's coffee shop that offers pastries, cheesecakes, bagels, muffins and cookies, in addition to a variety of coffees. Bulldog Café offers pizza, salads, sandwiches, hamburgers, and Chick-fil-A for lunch. They accept cash, credit cards, and UGA cards. (You can put money on your UGA card.) Also, there is a little lunch/coffee spot called Favorite near Oglethorpe Dining Commons where students can find sandwiches, candies, coffees, smoothies, teas, bakery goods, and fruit.

Did You Know?

The dining halls have a day at the end of the year when they request that students **return all stolen silverware to each cafeteria**. This event has, surprisingly, been a huge success in recent years.

UGA Food Services has **received 52 national awards for their excellence** in student meal plans.

Students Speak Out On...
Campus Dining

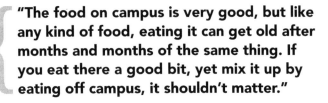

"The food on campus is very good, but like any kind of food, eating it can get old after months and months of the same thing. If you eat there a good bit, yet mix it up by eating off campus, it shouldn't matter."

Q "The on-campus food is very good. I lived in the dorms for two years and have a lot of experience in this area. There are four main dining halls, and many agree that Snelling is the best one, offering made-to-order sandwiches of every kind. Bolton and Oglethorpe both provide full-course meals and salad bars. The Village East was built in 2004 and is also very popular, but at times, it gets very crowded. **The dining halls occasionally offer theme nights** where shrimp kabobs and luau-type foods are served."

Q "**Food on campus is just cafeteria food, but it's good**. You can get different kinds of sandwiches hot off the grill. You can get pizza. You can use the salad bar. Then, you can still get the different entrée that they have each night. Each dining hall offers different things on different nights, so you just have to know what you can get at each place. There are four different dining halls on campus: Snelling, Bolton, Oglethorpe, which is sometimes called O-House, and Village East. They are all good, but I always went to Snelling. It was just my personal favorite."

Q "To be honest, **the food from the dining halls really kind of sucks**. It isn't that bad, but it gets old after a while. There aren't many places to eat on campus besides the four dining halls."

Q "The food is pretty good. It's actually better than I thought it would be. There are four dining halls, but **Village East is the best**. You can have pretty much anything that you could want there, and that's where we usually go to eat. Bolton Hall is pretty good, too. All in all, the food is much better than I had expected."

Q "The **food on campus is amazing**. There is something for everyone, including extravagant foods such as tofu pizza, Philly cheesesteak sandwiches, salad bars, omelet stations, and ice cream tables with every topping imaginable. Whether you are in the mood to eat healthy or not, there is always something for you. Another nice feature is that the nutritional information of all the foods is available for you so you can know exactly what you're eating. The dining halls also have specialty days, on which the dining hall is specially decorated with themes like 'Beach Party,' 'Under the Big Top,' 'Tastes From Around the World' and 'Silver Platter Night.'"

Q "Personally, I find the food a bit bland, and sometimes **they mix leftovers with other leftovers and call it a new dish**. I don't feel like the meal plan saves much money on food or is a very healthy option. The highlight of the meal plan is Sunday brunch, especially the french toast sticks and the amazing desserts."

Q "**Some of the stuff at the dining halls is really gross**, like cod fillets. When that's the main course for the night, I just get cereal or make a waffle."

Q "I stayed on the meal plan after freshman year, because the food was pretty good and eating in the dining halls is **a good way to hang out and meet people**. Plus, I didn't want to have to cook."

Q "Around the end of the year, **you start to get really tired of some dining hall food**, but usually, it's not that bad."

Q "Dining hall food is fabulous. **Take advantage of the meal plan**. Everything you could imagine is available at one of the dining halls. The fourth dining hall, Village East, is amazing. Bulldog Café is one great place to eat and meet friends that is not a dining hall."

Q "I like the food, but it's not the main reason I eat at the halls. I like the dining halls because eating there is a chance to socialize. The ice cream is weird, but their other **desserts are usually delicious**."

Q "The people at the dining halls really try to come up with things they think we'll like, and **everyone is really cool**."

The College Prowler Take On...
Campus Dining

Most freshmen will be assigned to live in a high-rise dorm and will therefore be eating at Bolton a lot. Bolton has a great salad bar, and if grilled cheese and tomato soup is your thing, the dining experience will be comparable to heaven. However, the variety gets very old by second semester, and strange options, such as cod fillets, show up now and then. Snelling is definitely the best dining hall because of its made-to-order hot sandwiches and pizza buffet. It is usually packed with a line out the door at noon, but it's worth waiting for. Oglethorpe, known as O-House, is not very crowded during the week, but on Sundays it gets packed. The brunch is so good that local Athens residents, who are not students, choose to come to O-House after church. The Village Summit, adjacent to East Campus Village and Ramsey Center, has been a big hit with students since it opened in 2004. It has two levels and offers items students can pay cash for on the bottom floor, like a restaurant, with a dining hall on the top floor.

Each meal is about $3 when you have a meal plan. You get unlimited food each time you visit, and you can visit a dining hall as many times a day as you like. However, you cannot take food with you. If you live off campus, the parking situation makes it difficult to continue on the meal plan. However, if you are a freshman and live on campus, I would highly recommend getting on the meal plan.

B

The College Prowler® Grade on
Campus Dining: B

Our grade on Campus Dining addresses the quality of both school-owned dining halls and independent on-campus restaurants as well as the price, availability, and variety of food.

Off-Campus Dining

The Lowdown On...
Off-Campus Dining

Restaurant Prowler:
Popular Places to Eat!

Broad Street Bar & Grill

Food: American, full bar
Corner of Broad and Jackson streets
(706) 548-5187
Price: $8–$12
Hours: Monday–Saturday
11 a.m.–2 a.m.,
Sunday 11 a.m.–12 a.m.

Chili's Grill & Bar

Food: American
185 Alps Rd.
(706) 613-5405
Price: $7–$15
Hours: Monday–Thursday
11 a.m.–11 p.m., Friday–
Saturday 11 a.m.-12 a.m.,
Sunday 11 a.m.-11 p.m.

DePalma's Italian Café

Food: Italian, wine cellar
401 E Broad St.

→

(DePalma's, continued)

(706) 354-6966

Price: $15–$25

Hours: Sunday–Wedensday
11 a.m.–10 p.m.,
Thursday 11 a.m.–11 p.m.,
Friday–Saturday
11 a.m.–12 a.m.

East West Bistro

Food: Fusion cuisine, Northern
Italian, Seafood

351 E Broad St.

(706) 546-9378

Price: $20–$30

Hours: Sunday–Thursday
11a.m–10 p.m., Friday–
Saturday 11 a.m.–11 p.m.
Bar open daily 11 a.m.–2 a.m.

The Grill

Food: American (diner)

171 College Ave.

(706) 543-4770

Price: $5–$10

Hours: Open 24 hours

Five and Ten

Food: American gourmet

1653 S Lumpkin St.

(706) 546-7300

Price: $15–$25

Hours: Monday–Thursday
5:30 p.m.–10 p.m.,
Friday–Saturday
5:30 p.m.–11 p.m.,
Sunday brunch
10:30 a.m.–2:30 p.m.

Five Star Day Café

Food: Gourmet soul food

229 E Broad St.

(706) 543-8552

Price: $6–$12

Hours: Monday–Thursday
7 a.m.–10 p.m., Friday–
Saturday 7 a.m.–11 p.m.,
Sunday 10 a.m.–4 p.m.

The Grit

Food: Vegetarian

199 Prince Ave.

(706) 543-6592

Price: $5–$10

Hours: Monday–Wednesday
11 a.m.–9:30 p.m.,
Thursday–Saturday
10:30 a.m.–10:30 p.m.,
Saturday–Sunday
10 a.m.–3 p.m., 5 p.m.–10 p.m.

Gumby's Pizza

Food: Pizza

496 Baxter St.

(706) 543-5000

Price: $10–$15

Hours: Daily 11 a.m.–3 a.m.

Gyro Wrap

Food: Pita wraps

175 E Broad St.

(706) 543-9071

Price: $5–$10

Hours: Daily 11 a.m.–2 a.m.

Harry Bissett's New Orleans Café & Oyster Bar

Food: Steak and Seafood

279 E Broad St.

(706) 353-7065

Price: $15–$30

Hours: Monday–Thursday
7 a.m.–10 p.m., Friday–
Saturday 7 a.m.–11 p.m.,
Sunday 10 a.m.–8 p.m.

Inoko Japanese Steak and Seafood House

Food: Japanese

161 Alps Rd.

(706) 546-8589

Price: $10–$30

Hours: Lunch: Sunday–Friday
11:30 a.m.–2:30 p.m.; Dinner:
Sunday 4:30 p.m.–9:30 p.m.,
Monday–Thursday
4:30 p.m.–10 p.m., Friday–
Saturday 4:30 p.m.–10:30 p.m.

Johnny Carino's Country Italian

Food: Italian

3595 Atlanta Highway

(706) 613-1592

Price: $8–$25

Hours: Monday–Thursday
11 a.m.–10 p.m., Friday–
Saturday 11 a.m.-11 p.m.,
Sunday 11 a.m.-10 p.m.

Last Resort Grill

Food: Southern

184 W Clayton St.

(706) 549-0810

(Last Resort Grill, continued)

Price: $20–$30

Hours: Lunch: Monday–Sunday
11 a.m.–3 p.m.; Dinner:
Monday–Thursday
5 p.m.–10 p.m.,
Friday–Sunday 5 p.m.–11 p.m.

Little Italy

Food: Take out, pizza

125 N Lumpkin St.

(706) 613-7100

Price: $5–$15

Hours: Sunday–Thursday
11 a.m.–2 a.m., Friday–
Saturday 11 a.m.–4 a.m.

Loco's Deli & Pub

Food: Sandwiches, salads,
wings, bar

581 S Harris St.

(706) 548-7803

Price: $10–$15

Hours: Sunday–Saturday
11 a.m–12 a.m.

Mellow Mushroom

Food: Pizza

259 E Broad St.

(706) 613-0555

Price: $10–$15

Hours: Sunday–Saturday
11 a.m.–10 p.m.

On the Border Mexican Grill and Cantina

Food: Mexican

3640 Atlanta Highway

(On the Border, continued)

(706) 543-2299

Price: $10–$15

Hours: Monday–Thursday
11 a.m.–11 p.m., Friday–
Saturday 11 a.m.–12 a.m.,
Sunday 12 p.m.–10 p.m.

Outback Steakhouse

Food: Steaks

3585 Atlanta Highway

(706) 613-6015

Price: $10–$15

Hours: Monday–Thursday
4 p.m.–10:30 p.m.

Peking Restaurant

Food: Chinese

1935 Barnett Shoals Road

(706) 549-0274

Price: $12–$20

Hours: Lunch: Monday–Friday
11 a.m.–2:30 p.m.; Dinner:
Monday–Thursday
4:30 p.m.–10 p.m., Friday–
Saturday 4:30 p.m.–11:00 p.m.,
Sunday 11 a.m.–10 p.m.

Sons of Italy

Food: Italian

1573 S Lumpkin St.

(706) 543-2516

Price: $2–$7

Hours: Sunday–Saturday
11 a.m.–2 a.m.

Steverino's Pizza & Subs

Food: Pizza and subs

1583 S Lumpkin St.

(706) 353-7777

Price: $5–$10

Hours: Daily 11 a.m.–1 a.m.

Thai Café

Food: Thai

149 N Lumpkin St.

(706) 548-9222

Price: $8-15

Hours: Monday–Saturday
11:30 a.m.–3 p.m.,
5 p.m.–10 p.m.

The Varsity

Food: All-American

1000 W Broad St.

(706) 548-6325

Price: $5-$10

Hours: Monday–Thursday
10 a.m.–10 p.m., Friday–
Saturday 10 a.m.–12 a.m.

Wild Wing Café

Food: Wings

312 E Washington St.

(706) 227-WING (9464)

Price: $5–$15

Hours: Monday–Thursday
11 a.m.–11 p.m., Friday–
Saturday 11 a.m.–12 a.m.,
Sunday 12 p.m.–10 p.m.

Other Places to Check Out:
Barberito
Basil Press
Olive Garden
Panera Bread
Pita Pit
Quiznos
Waffle House

Student Favorites:
Five Star Day Café
The Grit

Grocery Stores:
Kroger
2301 College Station Rd.
(706) 353-8543

24-Hour Dining
The Grill

Best Food Specials:
Gumby's Pizza

Best Breakfast:
Five Star Day Café

Best Chinese:
Peking Restaurant

Best Healthy:
The Grll

Best Pizza:
Mellow Mushroom
Sons of Italy

Best Wings:
Wild Wing Café

Best Place to Take Your Parents:
Harry Bissett's New Orleans Café & Oyster Bar

Did You Know?

The Grit is owned by REM's Michael Stipe, who got the name for the band's album "Automatic for the People" from the slogan of another Athens restaurant, Weaver D's.

Students Speak Out On...
Off-Campus Dining

{ "Off-campus restaurants are great! The ones downtown are the best. My favorites are the Last Resort and East West. There are also some good fast food places around campus, too."

Q "Athens has an **incredibly large number of inexpensive restaurants**. Little Italy is a great pizza place downtown, and you can get a slice of pizza there for under $1.50. Taco Stand is another great downtown eatery, and of course you have to try the Georgia favorite, the Varsity on the corner of Milledge and Broad Street. Athens has an incredible variety of places at which to eat."

Q "The **restaurants off campus are even better than the ones on campus**. Downtown Athens is a wonderful place. You have to experience it to truly appreciate it."

Q "Some of **the more popular chain restaurants** are Johnny Carino's Country Italian, Loco's Deli & Pub, and Chili's Grill & Bar. Then there are the privately-owned restaurants, most of which can be found downtown. The atmosphere at all of these places is so fun and relaxing, plus, the food is amazing on top of it."

Q "There are **always new restaurants to try in Athens**, so you can pretty much find whatever you want. I know there is an Olive Garden everyone is excited about."

Q "**Downtown has restaurants to meet any craving**. There are familiar restaurants, such as Mellow Mushroom, but the best are those unique to Athens. Five Star Day Café, Basil Press, and Broad Street Bar & Grill are just a few of the many tasty restaurants."

Q "I have been to so many great restaurants in Athens, and that's actually **where most of my money goes, to eating out at restaurants**. My favorites are Gumby's Pizza and Pita Pit."

Q "**Little Italy has great pizza when you're drunk**. I always crave it. Wild Wing Café is good, and Quiznos is quickly becoming one of my favorites, as well."

The College Prowler Take On...
Off-Campus Dining

Off-campus dining is pretty decent. There are a large number of ethnic restaurants offering Chinese, Jamaican, Japanese, Thai, Mexican, and Italian foods. Downtown has some very nice restaurants for your parents to take you, as well as many cheaper, more casual spots. Five Star is very popular for lunch and dinner, and so are places like Panera and Barberito's. For late-night munchies, you can get a milkshake at the Grill downtown, and you can bet there will be students hanging out in the Waffle House at any given hour of the day or night. Gumby's Pizza is great for late-night munchies, because it's located across the street from the high-rise dorms and open very late.

Really, if you can't find what you're looking for here, there are hundreds of restaurants that are worth the hour drive to Atlanta. It's actually a fun date if you make the drive to Atlanta for dinner.

The College Prowler® Grade on

Off-Campus Dining: B+

A high off-campus dining grade implies that off-campus restaurants are affordable, accessible, and worth visiting. Other factors include the variety of cuisine and the availability of alternative options (vegetarian, vegan, Kosher, etc.).

Campus Housing

The Lowdown On...
Campus Housing

Undergrads Living on Campus:
27%

Number of Dormitories:
17

Best Dorms:
East Campus Village
McWhorster
Myers
Oglethorpe House

Worst Dorms:
Creswell
Russell

Dormitories:

Boggs Hall

Total Occupancy: 161

Bathrooms: Community

Coed: Yes

Room Types: Double

Special Features: Recreation area, television room, study lounge, laundry, Wellness housing

Brumby Hall

Floors: 9

Total Occupancy: 950

Bathrooms: Community

Coed: No, women only

Room Types: Double

Special Features: Rotunda on ground floor with TV, aerobics room, laundry rooms on every third floor, kitchen on every floor, lounge for every hall, central heat/air, hand ID scanners at entrance, 24-hour desk attendant, elevators, computer lab

Church Hall

Total Occupancy: 160

Bathrooms: Community

Coed: No, women only

Room Types: Double

Special Features: Recreation area, high ceilings

Creswell Hall

Total Occupancy: 975

Bathrooms: Community

(Creswell Hall, continued)

Coed: Yes

Room Types: Double

Special Features: Television room on ground floor, elevators, 24-hour desk attendant on hand, separate air-conditioning units for each room, computer lab, guidance offices on ground floor

Hill Hall

Total Occupancy: 165

Bathrooms: Community

Coed: Yes

Room Types: Double

Special Features: Recreation area, television room, study lounge, laundry

Lipscomb Hall

Total Occupancy: 158

Bathrooms: Community

Coed: Yes

Room Types: Double

Special Features: Recreation room, television room, study lounge, laundry, computer cluster, mail room, common kitchen area

Mary Lyndon Hall

Total Occupancy: 121

Bathrooms: Community

Coed: Yes

Room Types: Single, double

Special Features: Foreign language dorm

McWhorter Hall
Total Occupancy: 218
Bathrooms: In-room
Coed: No, men only
Room Types: Double
Special Features: Student athlete dorm

Mell Hall
Total Occupancy: 161
Bathrooms: Community
Coed: No, women only
Room Types: Double
Special Features: Lounge, reading/study room

Morris Hall
Total Occupancy: 144
Bathrooms: Community
Coed: Yes
Room Types: Double, double in suite
Special Features: Air conditioned, television room, computer cluster, mailroom

Myers Hall
Total Occupancy: 404
Bathrooms: Community
Coed: Yes
Room Types: Double, double in suite, single in suite
Special Features: Students love the Myers quad

Oglethorpe House
Total Occupancy: 504
Bathrooms: Semi-private

(Oglethorpe, continued)
Coed: Yes
Room Types: Double in suite, single in suite
Special Features: Located right next to Oglethorpe dining hall, very close to many classes

Payne
Total Occupancy: 197
Bathrooms: Community
Coed: No, women only
Room Types: Single, double
Special Features: Lounge, laundry

Reed Hall
Total Occupancy: 296
Bathrooms: Semi-private
Coed: Yes
Room Types: Single, double, double in suite
Special Features: Air conditioned, lounge

Russell Hall
Total Occupancy: 975
Bathrooms: Community
Coed: Yes
Room Types: Double
Special Features: Television lounge on ground floor, computer lab, ATM machine, elevators, central air/heat, elevators, 24-hour desk attendant on hand

www.collegeprowler.com

Rutherford Hall

Total Occupancy: 153

Bathrooms: Community

Coed: Yes

Room Types: Single, double

Special Features: Air conditioned, television room, computer cluster, mailroom

Soule Hall

Total Occupancy: 95

Bathrooms: Semi-private

Coed: No, all female

Room Types: Single, double in suite, double in super-suite

Special Features: Lounge, laundry

Room Types:

Most rooms are double occupancy with bathrooms at the end of the hall. Older dorms have suite-style rooms with four to six people sharing a bathroom connecting two rooms. O-House has double occupancy rooms with a bathroom for every two rooms.

Bed Type

Twin extra-long (39" x 80"); most are bunkable, all are loftable

Cleaning Service

There is cleaning in public areas; staff cleans community and semi-private bathrooms several times a week. Carpeted halls and student lounges are regularly vacuumed.

What You Get

Rooms come with a bed, desk and chair, bookshelf, dresser, closet or wardrobe, window blinds, cable TV jack, Ethernet or broadband Internet connections, free campus and local phone service, and free access to UGA's movie channel. Bunk beds are also free on request.

Available for Rent

Mini-Fridge, microwaves, lofts. Available for purchase on move-in days are dorm-size carpet, lofts (can even be set up for you), and posters.

Students Speak Out On...
Campus Housing

{ **"The dorms are a lot of fun, but you lose a lot of privacy, which I thought was kind of hard to deal with. You'll meet lots of people, though. It's almost impossible not to."**

"I'll just give the basic gist of the dorms. Russell has 10 floors and is coed by hall, and there is always someone to party with. It's a great place, in my opinion. Creswell has nine floors, and is coed by floor. It's a little bit rundown, but still fun. Brumby has nine floors and is an all-girls dorm. I enjoy hanging out with guys a lot, so I wouldn't want to live there, but some of my friends did, and they loved it. Mell Hall, Lipscomb Hall, Hill Hall, Church Hall and other places are smaller, usually comprised more of upperclassmen, and are a little more boring. I wouldn't recommend living in any of those places if you don't like a lot of quiet. My advice to you is that you **choose Russell, Creswell, or Brumby**, although the rooms are smaller."

"The **dorms are decent, but the social life there is incredible**, to say the least. For freshmen, I recommend Russell. It is a coed dorm that houses around 1,000 students. The rooms are small, but you can loft the beds and do other things to make more space. You will meet amazing people there, also. For all-female living, Brumby is located next to Russell and houses around 900 girls. The only dorm I would avoid is Creswell. It is older and just not as nice as the others."

"The **dorms at UGA are definitely a good way to start off your college career**. They are a great way to meet people, and they help you get used to your new college environment much easier."

Q "Brumby is all girls. That's not my thing, but a lot of my friends loved it there. Russell is very nice, but sometimes it's hard to get into, since everyone wants to live there. Creswell, called the 'Well,' is one of the oldest dorms on campus. Everyone dogs on it, but the best part about living in Creswell is that, **unlike the other dorms, you can control your room's heating and air-conditioning**."

Q "The **dorm life is a must for incoming freshmen**. It is the best way to meet people and get settled into a new life in Athens. You meet people that are going through the same things you are—leaving your family, deciding on a major, the anxiety of meeting new people, and so on. There are also some disadvantages of dorm life, like sharing bathrooms, less privacy, small rooms, waiting for elevators, and central air."

Q "**Avoid Creswell**! If you can, try to get something besides Brumby and Russell. They have really small rooms."

Q "The **dorms are alright, but not that great**. They're pretty small, but you can make do. Russell, Creswell, and Brumby are the ones most freshmen live in, so any of those would be good for a new student."

Q "I had so much fun living in the dorms. It was kind of terrifying at first, because there were people I didn't know everywhere I looked. But my hall was awesome, and once we got to know each other, it was a lot of fun. **There was always something crazy going on in someone's room**, kind of like having a big slumber party every night."

Q "The **dorms are a great community for students**. There is a variety of sizes of dorms to meet your comfort. While you are sharing a room, it is an experience like no other. I recommend that all freshmen take advantage of the living situation by getting involved on campus and meeting new people."

The College Prowler Take On...
Campus Housing

Each hall has an RA whose two sole purposes in life are to answer any questions residents have, and to try to keep order in the building—neither being an easy task. Each hall has its own parties and socials every so often, and there is definitely a sense of community within every hall. And, get this—the bathrooms are usually very clean, except during football game weekends. One time, a bathroom in Creswell was shut down because it had become a biological hazard over one weekend, which is gross, but it was up and running by Monday. The maintenance staff in the dorms are very nice, as well. All the dorms now have air-conditioning. If you are lucky enough to have an individual unit in your room, like Creswell residents for example, count your blessings. The dorms with central air are usually on the warm side. You can open your windows, but this does not always help.

The Myers, Rutherford, and Mary Lyndon quad is a very popular place to hang out and play ultimate Frisbee. Even before renovations, Myers was a very popular dorm. It is also close to Snelling, which is a big plus. If you live in an all-female dorm, especially Brumby, it can seem to be overrun with sorority girls at times. Many people complain that they feel like they are the only girls on campus who didn't rush. The East Campus Village was designed to resemble apartments in an effort to keep students on campus. They offer 1,200 beds, and preference is given to students who have spent the most time in a dorm.

B-

The College Prowler® Grade on

Campus Housing: B-

A high Campus Housing grade indicates that dorms are clean, well-maintained, and spacious. Other determining factors include variety of dorms, proximity to classes, and social atmosphere.

Off-Campus Housing

The Lowdown On...
Off-Campus Housing

Undergrads in Off-Campus Housing:
73%

Average Rent:
$305-$325 per bedroom

For Assistance:
Athens Apartment Blue Book
www.apartmentbluebook.com

Best Time to Look for a Place:
Beginning of second semester

Popular Areas:
Riverbend Road (Riverbend Club, Aspen, and College Park), River Club, River Mill, Whistlebury and Campus Lodge are close to downtown and North Campus. Polo Club and the Reserve are on the East side of Athens.

Students Speak Out On...
Off-Campus Housing

"There are so many off-campus housing options that it will make you dizzy. There are apartments ranging from $250 a month to $500 a month."

Q "Athens is a great college town, so naturally, **there are tons of off-campus apartments**, houses, duplexes, and lofts at which to live; many of which are within walking distance to campus. Next year, I am living in a duplex with five of my friends (three on each side of the house). Each side will have a room for everyone and two bathrooms, plus a huge backyard overlooking a large creek in the woods, and a beautiful front yard and porch. We are a mere six-minute drive from campus, and I will be paying only $285 a month!"

Q "There are **plenty of apartments, houses, and other housing options**, all located right around campus and offering great prices. Many are on the bus line. For example, I lived in a four-bedroom, two bathroom apartment less than a mile from campus and I paid $289 a month. The building was fully furnished with a pool, a computer lab, and a work-out area, so off-campus housing is very affordable."

Q "**Living off campus is basically essential after your freshman year**. Not many people live on campus after their freshman year, and there are tons of available apartments off campus."

Q "It depends on where off campus you want to live. **Most off-campus housing is pretty convenient** because they have an Athens transit line that runs all over town. You just have to know which bus goes where. There is housing off campus that is within walking distance to campus, but it all depends on how much money you want to pay for rent."

Q "Although dorm life was well worth it, **living off campus is also another experience you should have in college**. It does make it more time consuming to get on campus for class, but I think it is well worth it. You are able to have more people over, and more space."

Q "Housing off campus has its good and bad points. It is definitely further from campus than any of the dorms, which presents a few problems. The problem of commuting becomes a bigger issue because you have further to go. **You need to allot more time for your commute**, and oftentimes, you have to take the city bus, as opposed to the campus buses. On the plus side, though, you do have much more space, including your own room and oftentimes, your own bathroom. For people who want more space, off-campus housing is probably a good choice, but for people who don't mind the smaller quarters and need less personal space, the dorm would be a better choice."

Q "After my freshman year, I moved off campus and it was great for awhile before I realized I needed to commute to campus like four times a day. If you're going to live off campus, **I would recommend living in an apartment close to campus**."

Q "Off-campus housing is a welcome change after living in the dorms. **I was definitely ready for my own bedroom and bathroom** after a year in the dorms."

Q "There are numerous apartments. Some are close enough to walk to campus. Many of them are on the bus lines to get to campus, or parking passes are available. **They are worth living in after you have experienced the dorms**. They provide the freedom of personal space."

Q "The best part about living off campus is that **you can throw big parties**. Parties always get busted sooner or later in the dorms, but they hardly ever get busted at apartments, even if people are standing around outside and down the block."

Q "**Off-campus housing is pretty cheap**, and you can get your own room and your own bathroom, which is really nice. Commuting to campus kind of sucks, though."

The College Prowler Take On...
Off-Campus Housing

Since 2004, students at UGA are required to live in the dorms as freshmen, but even before that, most freshmen chose to live on campus anyway. There are many apartment options for students. Most complexes are designed with students in mind, and offer individual leases, so there is minimal arguing among roommates as to how much each owes in rent. You can find one-, two-, and three-bedroom apartments all over town. Sometimes, each bedroom has its own private bathroom, and sometimes two people will share a bathroom. The rooms are not all the same size in some apartments, which can lead to problems.

Many complexes offer fully-furnished apartments, which is to say a sofa, kitchen table, chairs, beds, desks, bedside tables, and chest of drawers in each bedroom. You will still probably want to bring some furniture of your own. Many complexes also have a pool, small gym, tennis courts, a clubhouse with a pool table and television, and they normally have a small computer lab, as well. Also, there is often a bulldog motif permeating the grounds and clubhouses of apartment complexes, showing their school pride. Many complexes offer roommate-matching services and host socials every so often to encourage students to meet new people. Students who work at the apartment complexes can get discounted rent. The Athens Transit bus comes to many popular apartment complexes, so you don't necessarily have to buy a parking space, which can be pricey.

The College Prowler® Grade on
Off-Campus
Housing: A+

A high grade in Off-Campus Housing indicates that apartments are of high quality, close to campus, affordable, and easy to secure.

Diversity

The Lowdown On...
Diversity

African American:
6%

Native American:
Less than 1%

Asian American:
6%

White:
83%

Hispanic:
2%

Unknown:
1%

International:
Less than 1%

Out-of-State:
11%

Political Activity

There is a large following for the College Republicans, as well as among the Young Democrats. Both the Republicans and Democrats are very active, with both sides hosting lectures, participating in anti- or pro-war demonstrations, and speaking out to newspapers and students.

Gay Pride

The campus is not terribly accepting of gays and lesbians. Like any place, there are some students who are supportive of the gay community, and others who are not. There have been several demonstrations at the Tate Center surrounding this particular issue.

Most Popular Religions

There are a lot of very active Christian groups at UGA. Baptist groups probably have the largest numbers, though. Catholics are the smallest Christian group, and there are a significant number of Jewish students here, as well. There is a Jewish student center, as well as predominantly Jewish sororities and fraternities which students can join. Most religious activity takes place off campus at churches or places of worship that cater to college-age people.

Economic Status

UGA has students from diverse economic backgrounds, but there seems to be a predominant amount coming from wealthy families. It seems like everyone you meet is from Atlanta, and drives a Land Rover. However, the HOPE scholarship has changed the composition of UGA for the better, allowing large numbers of middle- and lower-income students the opportunity to come here.

Minority Clubs

UGA has African American and Asian sororities and fraternities. UGA also offers minority students the opportunity to join the Abeneefoo Kuo Honor Society, Black Affairs Council, Hispanic Student Association, Indian Cultural Exchange, and Pamoja Dance Company.

Diversity

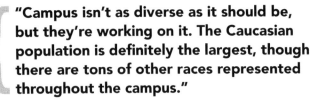

"Campus isn't as diverse as it should be, but they're working on it. The Caucasian population is definitely the largest, though there are tons of other races represented throughout the campus."

Q "The **campus has a decent minority population**, but lags a little in black student attendance because Atlanta is 60 miles away, and has three of the top five predominantly African American schools in the country. As far as the other races go, it's a little low, but we have formidable Hispanic and Asian populations."

Q "The campus is actually not that diverse. **There are some minority groups at UGA, but very few of them**. Most of the people here are white. The minorities that do go here are generally accepted and looked upon as equals. If you've heard that the South can be very racist, don't be worried about that. Although there is the occasional person who is racist, most of the people who I've met are not."

Q "I'm not going to lie to you, it's not very diverse. **Most of the kids are upper-middle class and white**. UGA is quite lacking in diversity. A whole lot of the kids are from the Atlanta area, or from somewhere in Georgia, mostly because of the HOPE scholarship, which is given to Georgia high school students who maintain a GPA of 3.0 or higher, and in return, HOPE pays for a student's in-state tuition."

Q "It's no secret that **UGA isn't that diverse**, but I think the numbers are getting better."

Q "Racially, the campus isn't as diverse as others, though it seems like it's pretty diverse to me. **About 15 percent of campus is comprised of minorities**, but it seems like it's more diverse than that when you're walking around campus. Those are the statistics, though. I think that whatever the actual percentages might be, it doesn't matter. Everyone seems to get along, and there are enough events organized by minority groups that everyone can participate in."

Q "I am not white, and I don't really think UGA is very diverse; it's **definitely not as diverse as it claims**. Maybe it's just stereotypical of me to say, but I feel like there are a lot of Southern, narrow-minded people here. But on the same token, there are many embracing people."

Q "The campus is really not diverse at all. It's almost all white. **There is a small black population**, but I would say it's maybe five percent."

Q "I don't think the campus is very diverse, but **I always read stories in the paper** about how the administration is trying to recruit minority students and improve diversity, so hopefully it will get better."

Q "Honestly, the campus is not very diverse. **The graduate program is more diverse than the undergraduate**. There are several ethnicities represented throughout the school, but overall, most of the students are Caucasian."

Q "**Most of my TAs have been Asian**, and I know a few African American students here, but there's definitely a white majority. I've heard racist comments on campus and downtown a couple of times, and there is definitely the 'Old South' mindset in some students, but being white, I guess I don't know exactly how big a problem that is."

The College Prowler Take On...
Diversity

There is not a lot of diversity on UGA's campus. Considering that the state population of Georgia is about 30 percent black, the fact that only 5 percent of UGA's student population is African American is, perhaps, a reason for concern. A new program called the African American Male Initiative has been instituted to improve diversity on campus. With this program, black high school and middle school students will be targeted and guided by counselors and other educators on which school is best for them. There is, however, a noteworthy number of Asian and Indian students on campus. Many TAs and professors are of Asian or Indian descent, as well. And even though the Hispanic population in Georgia is growing rapidly, the Hispanic student population at UGA has remained consistently under five percent over the years.

There is a lot of Old South spirit alive at UGA—many fraternities still fly the Confederate flag every now and again. Because UGA is so predominantly white, this is a fairly common theme. People are not usually racist, but the undercurrent is still there. The good news is that the minority students and clubs on campus seem to be very involved and close-knit. In conclusion, a student's social circle at UGA could be composed of all walks of life, but they should keep in mind that the path they'll be treading on will ultimately lead through the Deep South.

The College Prowler® Grade on

Diversity: D-

A high grade in Diversity indicates that ethnic minorities and international students have a notable presence on campus and that students of different economic backgrounds, religious beliefs, and sexual preferences are well-represented.

Guys & Girls

The Lowdown On...
Guys & Girls

Male Undergrads:
42%

Female Undergrads:
58%

Birth Control Available?
Yes, at the University Health Center, birth control prices vary depending on the type and quantity of birth control purchased. For some prescriptions, purchasing a three-month supply is cheaper than purchasing for one month. Also, costs from the pharmacy do not include a physical exam that may be required for the prescription.

Social Scene

There are unlimited opportunities to meet people at UGA: on the bus, at the Student Learning Center, in any class, during group projects, in Greek organizations, in clubs, at the library, at sporting events, at coffee shops, and of course, downtown.

Hookups or Relationships?

Many people are in stable relationships, but there is a huge pool of singles out there. Hookups occur rampantly at the bar scene downtown and at football games. Because alcohol is so popular, the walk of shame is pretty common for many students. Almost everyone is looking for romance in some capacity.

Best Place to Meet Guys/Girls

The best places to meet people are downtown Athens and at fraternity parties. Any bar or frat party is bound to be packed with students looking for a good time. People are drunk, well dressed, and are looking to hook up. Many students get dressed up to go out, so there are a lot of beautiful people in Athens.

The coed dorms are also great places to meet members of the opposite sex. Usually, the male floors will have some kind of party going on, and watching late-night movies on the futon is very common.

With a little maneuvering, the dining halls and libraries can serve as a dating medium, too. Proper seating arrangements are key, but this is not a tough obstacle to overcome.

Dress Code

During the week, students wear shorts, tank tops, flip-flops, and T-shirts to class. Some people even wear pajamas. It gets really hot outside, especially if you have to walk fast up a hill to class, so minimal clothing is really a good idea.

On game days, it's all red and black everywhere you look. Red pants are extremely popular for guys and girls, and you'll find that most of the stores in Athens stock red and black clothing for game days.

To go out, most people get dressed up. Many girls will wear designer clothing and stiletto heels downtown. Skimpy little skirts and dresses are always popular. Guys get dressed up, too, but in more of an Abercrombie sort of way.

Did You Know?

Top Three Places to Find Hotties:

1. Downtown
2. Frat parties
3. Dorms

Top Places to Hook Up:

1. Frats
2. Dorms
3. Downtown
4. Football games
5. Off-campus parties

Students Speak Out On...
Guys & Girls

"The guys here are hot, but it seems like they're all taken by beautiful girls. A guy once said that if you threw a rock into a crowd, you would hit a hot girl."

"The **girls on this campus are the most gorgeous girls** that a man will ever encounter in his life. I can make this claim after having visited a lot of different schools."

"**Most of the guys are gentlemen**, but there are those who think that they're God's gift to women. I've met too many of those."

"**Guys at Georgia are very good-looking**. It seems like everywhere you look there's a cute guy, but we have our fair share of ugly guys, too."

"Girls here are cute, or so I've been told, but **Georgia has a reputation for having very pretty girls**."

"Most of the guys are good old Southern boys. They drink too much, **they're too loud, and sometimes they're way too horny**, but that's why we love them. Girls around Georgia are very friendly, for the most part. Southern people, overall, are pretty nice."

"The **girls here are amazing**. I'll be honest with you—one of the main reasons I came to school here is because the girls here are hotter than anything I've ever seen, and I'm coming from Atlanta. You will not find hotter girls anywhere else, trust me. Not only are they hot, but many of them are really easy!"

Q "The **guys are very nice, laid-back**, motivated and fun. The girls are down-to-earth, eager to help, and very approachable."

Q "Most **guys are nice**, and there actually are a few real gentlemen here."

Q "The **people here are great**. Most of them are easy to get along with, and I made friends very easily. Living in the dorms helps a lot. Most of the people here are very good looking, so that's a plus."

Q "I would have to say most people here are very good-looking. **There are a lot of fake tans and highlights on guys and girls**, and there are definitely girls that go overboard on makeup, but there are a lot of girls who are just naturally beautiful walking around campus."

Q "There are, of course, **many attractive students** since the campus is so large."

Q "**Everyone here seems to wear the same thing**, and it's really annoying—golf shirts and Rainbows (flip-flops) for guys, and sorority shirts and short black skirts for girls, and that's it."

Q "You **can't walk down the street without seeing an amazingly hot girl** here—it's ridiculous. Athens also has a pretty large population of easy girls."

Q "**Everyone here is beautiful**. I was actually shocked when I first started going here, because everywhere I went, there were beautiful people. Most of the guys are really sweet—when they're not drunk."

Q "When I show pictures of my friends at UGA to my family and people at other schools, they can't believe how good-looking everyone is. I don't really notice it any more, but I guess **most people here are pretty attractive**."

The College Prowler Take On...
Guys & Girls

Most students at UGA are very good-looking and friendly. There are a lot of tan, toned bodies walking around campus and downtown. Students have been classified as easygoing and down-to-earth, making it at least fairly easy to talk to people on and around campus. Going downtown is always a fashion show, since everyone usually looks their best when out on the town. Working out and sunbathing are very popular pastimes, so I guess it's only natural that the general population looks great. Because so many people are from Atlanta, the student body generally reflects the popular styles and trends.

There is definitely a classic frat boy look at UGA that involves the shorter, non-baggy shorts, Rainbow flip-flops, and collared, brightly-colored golf shirts. This, coupled with mop-top hair—that has not been cut since they left home—is pretty standard for many guys. T-shirts and shorts are pretty standard for most of the year, because it's so hot in Athens. Once it gets cold, though, everyone will have black pants and peacoats on with some kind of boots to match—because students need to stay trendy during all seasons.

The College Prowler® Grade on
Guys: A-

A high grade for Guys indicates that the male population on campus is attractive, smart, friendly, and engaging, and that the school has a decent ratio of guys to girls.

The College Prowler® Grade on
Girls: A+

A high grade for Girls not only implies that the women on campus are attractive, smart, friendly, and engaging, but also that there is a fair ratio of girls to guys.

Athletics

The Lowdown On...
Athletics

Athletic Division:
NCAA Division I

Conference:
SEC

School Mascot:
Bulldog

Men Playing Varsity Sports:
290 (3%)

Women Playing Varsity Sports:
239 (2%)

→

Men's Varsity Sports:

Baseball
Basketball
Cheerleading
Cross country
Football
Golf
Soccer
Swimming and diving
Track
Tennis

Women's Varsity Sports:

Basketball
Cheerleading
Cross country
Equestrian
Golf
Gymnastics
Soccer
Softball
Swimming and diving
Tennis
Track
Volleyball

Intramurals:

Arena Football
Basketball
Dodgeball
Final's 5K Race
Flag Football
Golf

(Intramurals, continued)
Racquetball
Soccer (indoor and outdoor)
Softball
Squash
Tennis (singles and doubles)
Ultimate Frisbee
Volleyball
Wiffleball

Club Sports:

Badminton
Baseball
Chinese Shao-Lin
Crew
Cricket
Cycling
Dodgeball
Equestrian
Fencing
Ice hockey
Integrated fighting
Judo
Kali
Karate (Tae Kwon Do)
Lacrosse
Powerlifting
Racquetball
Rugby
Sailing
Soccer
Ultimate Frisbee
Volleyball
Water Polo
Waterskiing
Wrestling

Getting Tickets

Getting football tickets can get quite complicated. For season tickets, students scan their student IDs and pay for the tickets in the spring, but don't pick up the actual tickets until the fall. For away tickets, students have their IDs scanned and are put into a lottery for each game. E-mails are then sent out to tell you if you have been chosen to recieve tickets for that game. You pay for and receive the away tickets in the fall. Freshmen have their own lottery for home games—some get all the home games, while others recieve only three games. The SEC Championship game was done by lottery, as well. Season football tickets cost around $45. Basketball season tickets are about $25, and you will pay for them and pick them up the same day. Tickets to any other event are under $5 per event—often free—and should not be a problem to get at the gate.

Most Popular Sports

On the varsity level, the football and basketball teams have the largest presence on campus. All of the IM sports are also very popular. Soccer and baseball draw large numbers, and ultimate Frisbee has a cult following.

Most Overlooked Teams

Baseball, hockey, swimming, tennis, soccer, volleyball—basically everything besides football and basketball are overlooked. With the exception of gymnastics, most women's teams don't receive a lot of attention.

Best Place to Take a Walk

The trail at the intramural fields and the track on Milledge Avenue (it's the only street without hills, and there's a lot of Greek houses) are very scenic.

Gyms/Facilities

Intramural fields

Outdoor and indoor tennis courts

Ramsey Center

Students Speak Out On...
Athletics

{ **"Varsity sports are a part of life here. Just about everyone is involved in attending games, particularly football. Thousands of fans come to town for the entire weekend during football season."**

Q "**Varsity sports are huge on campus**. UGA wins the most national championships out of any school except Stanford. Our tennis, gymnastics, and swimming and diving teams are national champions almost every year. However, the lifeblood of the sports program is the football team. Our football team is usually one of the best teams in the country, and you would be hard-pressed to find someone at UGA who doesn't love the Bulldogs. Football season is one of the times at UGA when the most partying occurs. After a home football game, downtown Athens is incredible. Intramural sports are also very popular. You can find any sport that you could possibly want here."

Q "This is UGA! It's Bulldog country! **You better get out of town on football weekends if you don't like football**. It's a way of life, and the games are so much fun. I didn't like football until I started going to school at UGA. It's awesome, and it is always such a great experience!"

Q "Football rules at UGA, followed by basketball and baseball. **Swimming and gymnastics are pretty big**, mostly because our teams are excellent and win the national competitions frequently. You'd better get ready to learn how to tailgate for football games, though. Football game days are really fun. Everybody dresses in red and black!"

Q "**Intramural sports are huge at UGA**. I play basketball and soccer. We have everything here: softball, flag football, indoor and outdoor soccer, swimming, volleyball, ultimate Frisbee, basketball, racquetball, and every other IM sport imaginable. The Ramsey Center, which is the student work-out center, features two weight rooms, aerobics and gymnastics studios, yoga classes, six basketball courts, racquetball and squash courts, an indoor soccer gym, table tennis, volleyball, swimming pools, and an indoor track. Our intramural fields are also close to Lake Herrick, and offers such activities as canoeing, rowing, and fishing. Surrounding the lake are miles of off-road trails and dozens of softball, soccer, rugby, and football fields."

Q "Varsity sports are a huge part of life at UGA. Football is obviously the biggest and most popular sport. Watching football is one of the most exciting things you can do in Athens. Other varsity sports, such as basketball and gymnastics, are also very big. **UGA is definitely a school with tremendous school spirit**, and this is made very clear through our participation and involvement in our varsity sports."

Q "Varsity sports, namely football, are huge on campus. **Saturday afternoons in the fall are dedicated to Georgia Football**, and rightfully so. Tailgating is probably the thing I love most about this University."

Q "I love football. Every year when the season ends, I start counting the days until the next fall. I feel bad for the people who play other sports, because **they definitely don't get the recognition they deserve**."

Q "I have lived in Athens my whole life, and I have grown to hate football season, because **you can't go anywhere or do anything on game weekends**, and everyone is drunk and obnoxious."

Q "Football is obviously the biggest varsity sport, and thousands of people look forward to it every fall. I love it, but if you don't like sports, **you'll probably get sick of everyone's enthusiasm** real quick."

Q "My friends and I played intramural softball, basketball, and volleyball, and **we had a blast doing it**. It was a great way for us to hang out and do something different, besides drinking. We were not very good, but it was definitely worth doing."

Q "I feel bad, because I go to all the football games and maybe a few basketball games, but **I never go to any other sports**."

The College Prowler Take On...
Athletics

Football is God for many people at UGA. The alumni support is tremendous—they often show up in their RVs and trailers on Thursdays for a Saturday game. Alumni settle all over campus, and you will pass many of them grilling and drinking on your way to Friday classes, should you actually choose to go. Football games are the place to be on Saturdays, and many town businesses shut down until the weekend is over. Sanford Stadium holds more than 92,000 people, and it is almost always sold out or close to it. The other varsity programs have smaller followings and receive minimal press. Basketball games are a lot of fun and usually draw a decent crowd, and the band attends the games, so there's always that excitement and entertainment. Our women's gymnastics team is very good, and the gymnastics meets are becoming more and more popular with the student body and locals. Swimming is also pretty popular, as the teams consistently do pretty well, and the facilities are awesome.

Intramural sports are really popular for fitness and recreation. Some of the teams are really good, and others are just horrible. So you'll find your niche at any level if you are interested, and it seems like everyone has a lot of fun participating. Ramsey has excellent swimming, basketball, racquetball, and volleyball facilities, and the intramural fields are extensive. They include football and soccer fields, softball and baseball diamonds, tennis courts, walking trails, and even a large field for ultimate Frisbee players.

The College Prowler® Grade on

Athletics: A

A high grade in Athletics indicates that students have school spirit, that sports programs are respected, that games are well-attended, and that intramurals are a prominent part of student life.

Nightlife

The Lowdown On...
Nightlife

Club and Bar Prowler:
Popular Nightlife Spots!

The nightclubs in Athens are fantastic. They are usually pretty crowded any night of the week. The following are the best nightclubs in Athens that are usually filled with college students and people who wish they were still college students.

40Watt Club

285 W Washington St.
(706) 549-7871
www.40watt.com

This is a great club for concerts; it has standing room only. They are tough on fake IDs, but you only need to be 18+ to get in. Bars run along all sides of the dance floor. Tickets are usually $5–$10. Doors usually open at 10 p.m.

→

The Georgia Theatre

215 N. Lumpkin St.

(706) 549-9918

www.georgiatheatre.com

The GT is a large theatre that is great for bands and other shows. Athens' own The Damn Show, a local comedy act, often performs at GT. There is a large stage in front with standing room extending all the way back to the club entrance. You have to be 18 to get in, 21 to drink.

Cover: Range from $5–$25, depending on concert

Insomnia

131 E Broad St.

(706) 316-1000

Insomnia is a popular place for dancing. They play a lot of techno and dance music, and you can get in if you're 18. There are long lines to get in. Every week, there are different theme nights: including Flash back, hip hop night, and Drinkin' with Lincoln Night with one cent drinks all night.

Cover: Ranges, around $10

Bar Prowler:

Bars of all types are really popular in Athens. Downtown is always crowded, and it's always an interesting time. There is a particular special for every night of the week, too. Many bars are pretty easy to get into with a fake ID, but a few are definitely not.

For the most part, the following bars are very much alike: there's dance and hip-hop music blaring in the background, there are weekly specials, some people are dancing, others are hanging out. Most have some tables outside, as well as inside, and there are usually TVs in the corners with avid sports fans glued to them. They all check IDs at the door, and most even scan them. Most students don't stay at any single bar all night. There is a lot of bar hopping because there are hardly any cover charges in Athens.

Boar's Head

260 E Washington St.

(706) 369-3040

This bar has a great outdoor deck area that is always crowded because they cook cheeseburgers and fries outside, and people like to watch other drunk people walking around downtown. There is a Ping-Pong table downstairs and a big-screen HDTV.

Bourbon Street

333 E Broad St.

(706) 369-1313

Bourbon Street is a larger bar with a New Orleans theme that seems to be really popular with the ladies. It is always pretty crowded, and is fairly large compared to other bars.

City Bar

220 College Ave.

(706) 546-7612

City Bar is a classic bar with a slightly more sophisticated feeling. It is very popular with students, and is a popular place with Athens adults as well. There is a more intimate seating arrangement in City Bar than in other bars, and the décor is slightly more sophisticated, complimented by really high ceilings.

Classic City Saloon

335 E Clayton St.

(706) 227-6030

Classic City Saloon has a unique western theme, and a full bar for you to enjoy. Classic City Saloon offers two floors of great music, sometimes scandalous dancing, and of course, drinking.

The Firehouse

321 E Clayton St.

(706) 227-2007

(The Firehouse, continued)

The Firehouse is one of the most popular bars in Athens. There are lots of drink specials, including "power hour": one-dollar well drinks from 9 p.m.–10 p.m. every Friday. There is a big open space in the middle of the bar, instead of tables, so there are usually a lot of people dancing here.

Flannigan's

301 E Clayton St.

(706) 208-9711

Flanigan's is known for its St. Patrick's Day celebrations. Flanigan's also has a wide variety of drinks, including many beers on tap. Flanigan's Friday happy hour is very popular with students.

Last Call

420 E Clayton St.

(706) 353-8869

Last Call, formerly Athens Music Factory, is one of the largest of all the bars in Athens. There are weekly live music performances. There are also several pool tables, as well as darts and billiards.

Molly O'Shea's

430 E Clayton St.

(706) 227-2127

Molly O'Shea's resembles the atmosphere of a traditional Irish pub. Molly's offers a

(Molly O'Shea's, continued)

variety of drinks and beers, and is also known for its food, especially wings. Tuesday nights are ladies night with 50 cent well drinks. Thursday nights, you can get a free T-shirt with the purchase of a car- or Jaeger-bomb.

Washington Street Tavern

318 E Washington St.
(706) 613-7817

Washington Street is a great place to watch the Twilight bike race, or just to hang out. The $1 PBR's on Thursday at last call are very popular, and the bar plays a variety of music that everyone seems to know, and often people will be singing aloud together by the end of the night.

Other Places to Check Out:

El Centro

General Beauregard

The Globe

Toppers International Showbar

Student Favorites:

Boar's Head

City Bar

Georgia Theatre

Cheapest Place to Get a Drink:

The Firehouse

Molly O'Shea's

Washington Street Pub

Primary Areas with Nightlife:

Downtown

Bars Close At:

2 a.m.

Favorite Drinking Games:

Beer Pong

Card Games (A$$hole)

Quarters

Power Hour

Useful Resources for Nightlife

www.barsmart.com

www.flagpole.com
www.athensmusic.net

Organization Parties

Many clubs and Greek organizations will host events downtown. These events can range from disco dances to classy formal events. Because there are so many restaurants dispersed among the bars, it is very convenient to do dinner and drinks with groups.

What to Do if You're Not 21

The Dawgs After Dark program offers games, movies, guest speakers, and arcade games for students who are under 21, or who choose not to go downtown. Going to the movies and bowling are also popular. Bowling is cheaper after midnight. Hanging out at the dorm is always an option, as there will always be someone around to hang out with. All the dance clubs and concert venues allow 18-year-olds to enter.

AthFest is an annual event held downtown that is very popular for all ages. It is dubbed as a music and arts festival. There are outdoor concerts, a bar crawl, arts and crafts, an artist's market, and fun for kids up to adults. In the spring, there is a bike race around downtown Athens that locals and students flock to. It's really amazing to watch the cyclists speed around downtown, and people bring their dogs and kids to watch.

House Parties

House parties are usually very crowded, and the keg will often be floating before you even get there. Once people find out about a party, it's a mad dash to the keg. Polo Club Apartments hosts an annual block party with kegs at several apartments within the complex. This is a very popular event.

Frats

See the Greek section!

Students Speak Out On...
Nightlife

{ **"Athens is the best college town I've ever been to. Every bar and club in town caters to college students, and trust me, there are tons of them. I believe that there are over 30 bars, each with nightly drink specials."**

Q "You will always have a good club or bar to go to, and not only do **fake IDs come a dime a dozen in Athens,** but very few bars are strict about carding students."

Q "**Athens is known for its music scene**. It's been the birthplace of such acts as the B-52s, Widespread Panic, and REM. The past few years, Athens saw such acts as Ludacris, Pat McGee, John Mayer, Better than Ezra, REM, Blues Traveler, Dispatch, and tons more."

Q "The **bars in Athens rival those of any major city in which I have ever lived**. And, when I say major city, I mean cities such as Atlanta, Charlotte, Charleston, Orlando, Cincinnati, and Cleveland. Athens has a better bar scene than all of them. The only cities where it is better are heavy hitters like London, Amsterdam, Chicago, New York, and Los Angeles. I know that it's hard to believe, but visit Athens just once with a person who can take you to the right places, and you will know exactly what I am talking about."

Q "I love going out to the bars. **I could barely wait to turn 21 so I wouldn't have to worry** about getting caught with a fake ID. Now that I am legal, I go downtown several times a week. It's a great way to hang out and relieve some stress."

Q "The bars in Athens are so much fun. **There's no cover charge anywhere**, so it's fun to bar hop all night. You'll see people you know every time you're downtown, so it's always fun."

Q "Some places, like Clemson, have about two bars in the whole town, but Athens has probably 20 just downtown, so **you can really make a night of going out to the bars**."

Q "What's so great about downtown Athens is that **it's so cheap to get so drunk**. There are no cover charges, great drink specials, and cabs that are like $3, so you can get hammered for under $20, and go to as many different bars as you want."

Q "**You really have to have a good fake ID when you get to Athens**, because you're definitely going to want to go downtown. It's always a lot of fun, and there are concerts going on every week, if you really don't want to go to the bars."

Q "One of my favorite things to do from Thursday nights to Sunday afternoons is to go downtown. You can see anything from local acts to Dave Matthews cover bands, and the bars are so much fun because you can drink, dance, and socialize. **You will always see people you know downtown**."

Q "Freshmen with fake IDs can pretty much **plan on making bad grades their first semester**, because once they get a taste of the bar scene in Athens, it's going to be all they'll ever want to do."

Q "The bars in Athens are great. Some are really relaxed and casual, and others have loud music and dancing. **Whatever you're into, there's a bar you'll like**."

The College Prowler Take On...
Nightlife

The nightlife in Athens is wonderful. The bars have loud music, drink specials, and lots of people. It's like spring break every weekend, but with more clothes. There is always something going on downtown. There are great concerts and shows, as well. Students flock downtown almost every night of the week, particularly on Thursday through Saturday nights. There are specials every night of the week at different places, and these are usually written on chalkboards outside each bar. You will run into all kinds of people at bars and clubs, and it's always easier to meet people with a little alcohol running through your system, so chances are, you will probably make friends every time you go.

Last call is around 2 a.m., but people linger for another hour or so outside before they stumble home. Restaurants such as the Grill and Little Italy have great late-night drunk food. The nightlife is so good that more and more apartments are being built in proximity to the downtown area, so students can walk and not worry about having a driver or getting a taxi. If you do need a taxi, you can probably just flag one down on the street. It usually costs around $3 to $5 to get home. Parking can be a little tricky, but usually there are spaces in the decks available. There are bike cops out and about looking for minors in possession, so be careful not to put yourself in a bad position.

The College Prowler® Grade on

Nightlife: A-

A high grade in Nightlife indicates that there are many bars and clubs in the area that are easily accessible and affordable. Other determining factors include the number of options for the under-21 crowd and the prevalence of house parties.

Greek Life

The Lowdown On...
Greek Life

Number of Fraternities: 27	**Undergrad Men in Fraternities:** 20%
Number of Sororities: 22	**Undergrad Women in Sororities:** 25%

Fraternities:

Alpha Epsilon Pi
Alpha Gamma Rho
Alpha Kappa Lambda
Alpha Phi Alpha
Beta Theta Pi
Chi Phi
Delta Chi
Delta Tau Delta
Kappa Alpha
Kappa Alpha Psi
Kappa Sigma
Lambda Chi Alpha
Phi Gamma Delta
Phi Beta Sigma
Phi Kappa Psi
Pi Kappa Alpha
Pi Kappa Phi
Phi Delta Theta
Phi Kappa Theta
Phi Kappa Tau
Sigma Alpha Epsilon
Sigma Nu
Sigma Phi Epsilon
Sigma Pi
Theta Chi
Tau Epsilon Phi
Tau Kappa Epsilon

Sororities:

Alpha Chi Omega
Alpha Delta Pi
Alpha Gamma Delta
Alpha Kappa Alpha
Alpha Omicron Pi
Chi Omega
Delta Delta Delta
Delta Gamma
Delta Phi Epsilon
Delta Sigma Theta
Delta Zeta
Gamma Phi Beta
Kappa Alpha Theta
Kappa Delta
Kappa Kappa Gamma
Phi Mu
Pi Beta Phi
Sigma Delta Tau
Sigma Gamma Rho
Sigma Kappa
Zeta Phi Beta
Zeta Tau Alpha

Other Greek Organizations:

Interfraternity Council
Order of Omega
Panhellenic Council
Rho Lambda

Did You Know?

UGA offers **professional fraternities** in every college.

The all-fraternity average **GPA** is 3.07. The all-sorority average **GPA** is 3.33.

Students Speak Out On...
Greek Life

{ **"Greek life is pretty big here. Lots of girls rush sororities during freshman year, and some guys rush fraternities. They stick to themselves, but it's easy to have a great time while not being a member of one."**

Q "I wasn't interested in Greek life, but I went to high school an hour and a half away from UGA, and I already knew a few people there. You don't have to get involved with it, but if you are interested, **you should go through rush to find out more about it**. There is no reason to feel that if you don't get involved in Greek life, you won't meet people. That's simply not the case."

Q "I think something like **30 percent of the campus is involved in social sororities and fraternities**. I am in a professional fraternity, and there are many of those that you can join, but none of the Greek organizations dominate the social scene. UGA is a place where you won't ever feel pressured by the Greeks, but there is an adequate Greek scene if you decide you want to join. Either way, you won't lack social opportunities. Trust me!"

Q "Greek life is not as big as I thought it would be. I went through rush last year, but it was just not for me. UGA Greek organizations sponsor one of the most serious rush programs in the South, but **if you really want to be in a sorority or a fraternity, I would go through with it**. You will meet a lot of new people that way, but if you definitely know that you don't want to be in a sorority or a fraternity, you will not feel left out."

Q "I think that this is one of the most disappointing aspects of UGA—the Greeks rule. I went through rush, but never pledged. **The Greeks dominate the social scene**, more or less."

Q "When you first get here, it can seem like everyone is Greek, but after a while, **if you're not Greek, you'll get used to it**, and most likely, you'll have your own group of friends in no time."

Q "Sometimes, **I feel like there is actually a lot of animosity between Greeks and non-Greeks**. Anytime one Greek person does something wrong, people are so quick to write off the rest of us as drunken, party-crazy people. There are way more Greeks who contribute to charities, have good GPAs, and are upstanding people, than who are just screw-ups."

Q "**Greek life is a pretty large part of the school**, but it does not take over. There are plenty of students not involved in those organizations, as well. I don't mean to sound judgmental, but it is usually very easy to identify those that participate in the Greek organizations just by their appearances."

Q "**I have met nice Greeks, and not so nice Greeks**. It just depends on who you're with. When I was a freshman, it seemed like they dominated the social scene, but now, I don't really feel that way."

Q "I felt like the Greeks dominated campus when I was a freshman, but I don't really feel like that now. I think it's more that they are very visible, and by that, I mean they are **involved in all kinds of events on campus**, from student government to sports teams and intramurals."

Q "I went to a couple of frat parties, and I thought they were kind of lame. **The Greeks here are really enthusiastic**, and it kind of gets on my nerves sometimes."

Q "I love being part of the Greek community. I have met so many people who are now my best friends, and the socials are incredibly fun. I know girls who are snobby about it, but they make up a small percentage. **Most everyone is really nice once you get to know them**."

The College Prowler Take On...
Greek Life

Every night of the week, there is some Greek event going on, and the themes are really creative. If you have trouble meeting people and making friends on your own, you might want to consider rushing. You will meet literally hundreds of people, and there is great camaraderie within the community. Frat parties are very popular, and you don't have to be Greek to get in, but people do get turned away for various reasons. The Greeks can tend to dominate social life on campus at times, and if you live in an all-female dorm, there really is no escaping the incessant sorority news and gossip. Some of the Greeks are very stuck up and snobby and will not pay any attention to non-Greeks, but of course this does not apply to everyone.

Students hear all kinds of rush stories, ranging from the horrific to the ecstatic, but the students who are most disappointed are the ones who come into the process with their hearts set on a specific sorority or fraternity. Fraternity competition is generally not as fierce as that of sororities, but some students with all the proper recommendations and even legacies are still deferred from their top choices—it happens. Overall, if rushing is something you feel like you really want to do, there are tons of options, and you will probably find something you love. If you're undecided about the whole thing, talk to someone who has already done it. If you go into it with a few options, you will have much less stress.

A-

The College Prowler® Grade on

Greek Life: A-

A high grade in Greek Life indicates that sororities and fraternities are not only present, but also active on campus. Other determining factors include the variety of houses available and the respect the Greek community receives from the rest of the campus.

www.collegeprowler.com

Drug Scene

The Lowdown On...
Drug Scene

Most Prevalent Drugs on Campus:
Alcohol

Marijuana

Alcohol-Related Arrests:
433

Drug-Related Arrests:
20

Drug Counseling Programs

Advantage Behavior Health Systems

(706) 369-5745

Advantage Behavior Health Systems offers alcohol assessments, a risk reduction course for students, and treatment options.

Alcoholics Anonymous

(706) 543-0436

AA is a self-help group for students struggling with alcoholism.

Commencement Center

(706) 475-5797

The Commencement Center has many treatments available for students suffering from alcohol and drug related addictions.

Counseling & Psychological Services (CAPS)

(706) 542-2273

Psychologists team up to work with students suffering from alcohol or drug-related issues. Individual therapy sessions are also available by appointment.

Health Promotion Department

(706) 542-8690

The Health Promotion Department focuses on prevention and education. There are courses available concerning alcohol, tobacco, and drugs. Students can find support groups, counseling, intervention information, and there is also a health resource library available.

Medical Clinic

(706) 542-8666

The Medical Clinic conducts drug testing, and offers counseling for smokers trying to quit.

Students Speak Out On...

Drug Scene

{ **"Drugs are present at UGA. Obviously, alcohol is quite prevalent. I haven't seen much else, though, aside from marijuana. Stuff is available, but if you choose to 'say no,' people will not look down on you."**

Q "I can't really comment on the drug scene. **There is a lot of pot on campus**, although I don't know how much relative to other campuses. That's the only drug I really hear about. There are rumors of wealthy kids doing cocaine, but I don't personally know anything about that. I guess that if you look hard enough, you can find all kinds of drugs, but it's pretty easy to keep your nose clean."

Q "The drug scene is just like that of any other large campus. Pot is popular, and if you do it, that's cool, but if you don't, that's cool, too. I have friends who smoke pot and friends who don't. **Cocaine is actually pretty prevalent, but it's kept kind of quiet**. I know a few people who do it, but I myself would never get involved in that stuff, for obvious reasons. I've never felt pressured to use it, and it's not something to be worried about. You just have to think for yourself."

Q "I don't know much about the drug scene on campus. There's the occasional marijuana bust in a dorm room, and **I think a girl overdosed at a club as a result of doing too much ecstasy**. Otherwise, there isn't much of anything at all on campus."

Q "The drug scene here at UGA is pervasive. I've heard that **one of our dorms actually is rumored to be one of the 'top 10' pot-smoking dorms in the nation**. Alcohol is also a very big deal here. Athens has been called a 'drinking town with a football problem' to poke fun at the extreme amounts of alcohol consumed by crazed UGA football fanatics."

Q "**Drugs are pretty easy to come by** if you're interested. I've walked down my hall and noticed a particular scent seeping under the doors many times."

Q "Drugs here seem pretty common, I guess. I don't really hang out with many people that do drugs, but I would say **it's on par with any college as far as drug use**."

Q "I know people that do drugs, but **I would say alcohol is a much bigger problem** than cocaine or pot. If you get caught with drugs, especially in the dorms, you obviously get into a lot of trouble, and the penalties for alcohol are not as bad."

Q "I know kids that smoke pot and have done cocaine, and they obviously have buddies that do drugs with them, but **I think alcohol is a much bigger problem than drugs at UGA**."

Q "**Drugs are pretty common here**, and people get caught sometimes, but I wouldn't say it's a big problem or anything. It's college—you have to expect that kind of stuff."

The College Prowler Take On...
Drug Scene

Alcohol is probably the most abused substance on campus. There are lots of students, especially guys, who drink all the time. Drinking is one of the most popular pastimes at UGA. Alcohol is pretty easy to get no matter what age you are, and the excitement of downtown just encourages more drinking.

Smoking pot is pretty popular, but if someone is smoking in a dorm, he or she is usually caught pretty quickly. I have heard that Creswell Hall is one of the most common places people obtain and smoke pot. Cocaine is apparently fairly common on campus, as is ecstasy. I remember one time hearing about police finding Oxycontin in someone's dorm. None of these are big problems for UGA. You might hear a handful of stories involving these drugs in a whole year.

The College Prowler® Grade on

Drug Scene: C+

A high grade in the Drug Scene indicates that drugs are not a noticeable part of campus life; drug use is not visible, and no pressure to use them seems to exist.

Campus Strictness

The Lowdown On...
Campus Strictness

What Are You Most Likely to Get Caught Doing on Campus?

- Underage drinking
- Parking illegally
- Smoking pot in the dorms
- Making too much noise in your dorm
- Downloading copyrighted materials
- Trying to smuggle alcohol into football games
- Driving on Sanford Drive during weekdays

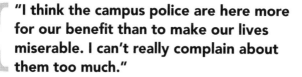

Students Speak Out On...
Campus Strictness

{ **"I think the campus police are here more for our benefit than to make our lives miserable. I can't really complain about them too much."**

Q "The campus police seem like jerks to most students, but I think that's because we're all college kids. So, naturally, we hate cops. I think that compared to cops elsewhere, **the campus police here are pretty lenient**. Every now and then, a kid gets busted for smoking weed in his dorm room, but then again, that's just a lack of common sense. People can drink in their dorms all the time, and on days when there are football games, open alcohol containers are permitted."

Q "Both **the campus and Athens police are pretty good about alcohol**. As long as you don't do anything stupid, like display an open alcohol container or pass out right in front of them, they won't usually hassle you about it. Do not drive while under the influence, or even after just one drink. If you get stopped, they will give you a breathalyzer test, and if you fail it, they haul you off to jail."

Q "Campus police are very liberal about drinking and drugs. **You just have to practice a certain degree of discretion**. If you act stupid and do stupid things, then you will get busted, but if you just keep it cool, you will have no problems."

Q "Campus police are only seen on rare occasions. I guess if you get into big trouble in the dorms, they become involved, but even then, **they try to deal with the problem in-house**."

Q "When the campus police does find drugs in the dorms, they, of course, have to crack down on security, but it's not like they monitor your every move or breathe down your neck. **They do their jobs.**"

Q "The campus police are **not really too strict with drug/ alcohol policies**. A lot just depends on the officer you happen to come into contact with. I've heard of a large number of people getting arrested or having their IDs taken away, but I've also heard of a lot of people getting by with just a warning. So, though the policies may suggest strict enforcement of the rules, I'm not sure that will always happen. On game days in particular, so many people are drinking that it would be near impossible to catch every underage drinker out there. So, I think the police admit defeat, and are particularly lax in these kinds of situations."

Q "I don't think the campus is all that strict on anything. You have to get permission to have demonstrations and stuff like that, but **you can pretty much protest or say anything you want to** with permission. Cops are out and about, but I wouldn't say they're just waiting for people to do something wrong."

Q "I do not have personal experience with this, but for the most part, **the police want you to be considerate of others**. If you are caught downtown underage with alcohol, consequences definitely follow."

Q "The thing that sucks about the campus police is if they catch you doing something, (as opposed to the Athens cops), **it gets reported in _The Red and Black_**. That can obviously be pretty embarrassing."

Q "The cops don't really come into the dorms unless there's something huge going on, so **the main person you'll have to deal with, and hide stuff from, will be your RA**. Most of them are cool, but I've heard of some that are real jerks."

The College Prowler Take On...
Campus Strictness

I think most students would agree that both campus and county police are pretty easy on college students. Unless you are acting completely belligerent or holding an open container right in front of a cop, you'll be fine. They definitely don't try to seek out troublemakers. They'd never get to sleep if they did. Most of the RAs will give you a warning if you are being too loud before they write you up or call the police. It's pretty lax around here no matter where you go. Getting caught with alcohol in the dorms is not a real big deal. You might have to take a class called OCTAA (On Campus Talking About Alcohol). Getting caught with drugs is more serious, whether on or off campus. Getting caught with a minor in possession (MIP) or an open container outside of campus will usually land you in court and eventually might lead to probation of some sort. People have gone to jail and usually have to appear in court if they are caught with drugs.

One thing to note is that on game days, people tailgate all over campus—from the dorm area to north campus to the parking lots by Ramsey. Open containers and underage-drinking laws apparently don't apply to anyone on such days. The cops will walk right by anyone with a beer in their hand, no matter where they are. But after the game, if you go downtown, I would not try to walk down the street with a beer. Also, smuggling alcohol into sporting events is prohibited. If you are caught, you will be thrown out of the game.

B+

The College Prowler® Grade on

Campus
Strictness: B+

A high Campus Strictness grade implies an overall lenient atmosphere; police and RAs are fairly tolerant, and the administration's rules are flexible.

Parking

The Lowdown On...
Parking

Approximate Parking Permit Cost:

From $10–$30 per month, depending on location. All deck spots are $30/month

UGA Parking Services:

325 River Rd.

(706) 542-7275

(706) 542-6301 (fax)

parking@uga.edu

Hours: Weekdays 8 a.m.–5 p.m.

Student Parking Lot?

Yes, many

Freshmen Allowed to Park?

Yes

Common Parking Tickets

Expired Meter: $10 at Ramsey deck
No Parking Zone: $15
Handicapped Zone: $75
Fire Lane: $25, automatically towed $65

Parking Permits

Faculty and grad students get priority selection for parking permits. Students living in the dorms are also given priority for lots near their dorms.

All undergrads put in a request online for their top three parking lot or deck choices. Permits are awarded by lottery, and students will receive a sticker or tag to indicate that they have a spot in a given area. There are many parking spaces on campus, but still not enough spots for everyone.

Did You Know?

Best Places to Find a Parking Spot
- Tate Center pay lot
- Broad Street
- Downtown
- Finley Street by the high-rise dorms

Good Luck Getting a Parking Spot Here!
- Baxter Street

The Boot!

If you accumulate three or more parking tickets, your car will be booted, and you will be unable to drive until you pay up.

Students Speak Out On...
Parking

{ **"Just about all parking on campus is designated for parking passes, which are available to students. There are several parking decks around the campus. In the evenings, parking is available to anyone."**

Q "**Parking is one of the biggest problems on campus**. It is extremely difficult to park and then walk to class. What most students tend to do is park at the parking decks and then take a campus bus to class. The bus ride usually takes about five minutes to get to anywhere on campus. I live fairly close to campus, so I just take one of the buses. Some areas immediately off campus, like mine for instance, have bus routes through them. I actually chose to live where I live because it's on the bus line."

Q "Parking is one of the biggest problems on campus, but then again, it's not really that bad. It's just that UGA is a big school, and as of right now, there are no rules, like some schools have, that prohibit certain people from bringing cars. I know that some schools don't allow freshmen to have cars. But, **the administration is constantly working on different ideas** to make sure that everyone who needs parking gets it."

Q "**Parking is a pain** on campus. That's one of the bad things about living here."

Q "Parking is kind of annoying. **They ticket very heavily**, and parking passes are very expensive. If you do buy one, though, they are very convenient."

Q "The parking scene on campus is somewhat chaotic. **You have to apply for a parking permit**, and a lot of times, you either don't get one at all, or you don't get the one that you want. If you are lucky enough to get the parking lots or deck of your choice, then parking is not really a problem for you. These spots do not necessarily come cheap, though, and can oftentimes cost over $150."

Q "I have been screwed by parking several times, and there's really nothing you can do about it. If you try to argue a ticket, even if you have a legitimate story, it doesn't really matter. **They'll flag your records**, and you won't be able to register for classes until you pay the fine."

Q "Parking is such a hassle sometimes. If you don't buy a deck or lot pass, which are really expensive, you either have to **park somewhere random** and walk up and down the Athens hills, or risk getting a fine for parking somewhere illegally."

Q "**There needs to be more parking at the SLC** for students. I can't tell you how many times I've been late to meetings and stuff because I couldn't find a place to park. Apparently, they are building a deck there to help the problem, but I'm sure it won't be done until after I graduate."

Q "If you're in a hurry and need to park (perhaps illegally), go downtown. **The tickets downtown are $3**, and on campus they're like $40, and downtown is adjacent to campus anyway."

Q "To get a pass to park anywhere decent is really expensive. I don't have that kind of money just to park. And the **parking people are always out trying to catch people parking illegally**."

The College Prowler Take On...
Parking

Parking is complicated. All undergraduates apply online for their top three lot or deck choices. Each lot and deck has a code, which can be found on the map on the Parking Services Web site. Permit prices vary according to the location of the space. No undergrad is guaranteed to get one of his or her top three choices, and for that matter, no undergrad is guaranteed to get any spot at all, but they do the best they can. A new deck was built at the East Campus Village that offers 850 spaces for students. Parking illegally is a common offense on UGA's campus. Parking Services religiously scours every lot and every floor of every deck several times a day to make sure the proper tags or stickers are displayed. If you park illegally, even for five minutes, there's a good chance you'll get caught.

Relying on just finding a random spot close to campus is not something I would recommend to anyone. If you live off campus and don't get a spot you like in the lottery, don't just assume you'll be able to find a street spot every weekday morning. After 5 p.m., you can park at the SLC—there is a free lot right next to it—or in the faculty lot behind the journalism building. The pay lot at the Tate Center does not charge students after 10 p.m. and is also close to the SLC.

The College Prowler® Grade on
Parking: C+

A high grade in this section indicates that parking is both available and affordable, and that parking enforcement isn't overly severe.

Transportation

The Lowdown On...
Transportation

Ways to Get Around Town:

On Campus
UGA buses run Monday–Friday
7 a.m.–12:30 a.m.

Public Transportation
Athens Transit
(706) 613-3430
www.athenstransit.com
Hours: Monday–Friday
6:15 a.m.–7:15 p.m., Saturday
7:30 a.m.–7 p.m.

(Athens Transit, continued)
Athens Transit buses travel through the major shopping locations and many neighborhoods, as well as into the University of Georgia campus and downtown.

Routes extend east to Lexington Road, west to Georgia Square Mall, and north to the Athens Area Technical Institute.

Taxi Cabs

A-1 Taxi Cab Services
660 W. Broad St.
(706) 546-0460
24-hour service
Airport shuttle available

Alfa Taxi
1121 Martin Luther King Jr. Pkwy.
(706) 583-8882
24-hour service
Airport transportation available

Your Cab Company
714 Oglethorpe Ave.
(706) 546-5844
Airport service, parcel pick up
and delivery

Car Rentals

Alamo
Local: (888) 426-3304
National: (800) 327-9633
www.alamo.com

Budget
Local: (706) 353-0600
National: (800) 527-0700
www.budget.com

Enterprise
Local: (706) 543-0771
National: (800) 736-8222
www.enterprise.com

Hertz
Local: (706) 543-5984
National: (800) 654-3131
www.hertz.com

Rent a Wreck
(706) 353-7325

Ford Rental System
(706) 546-8144

Jefferson Motor Co.
(706) 367-5217

Toyota Rent a Car
(706) 549-7002

Best Ways to Get Around Town

Athens is a car-friendly and bike-friendly town. Downtown parking is limited, so carpooling is a good idea if you're going in a group. Bikes are great for getting around quickly, and many major roads have bike lanes. The bus is the main option for people choosing public transportation. On campus, it's sometimes faster just to walk rather than catch what is sure to be a crowded bus.

Ways to Get Out of Town:

Airport

Hartsfield Atlanta
International Airport

www.atlanta-airport.com

Airlines Serving Atlanta

AeroMexico
(800) 237-6639
www.aeromexico.com

America West Airlines
(800) 235-9292
www.americawest.com

American Airlines
(800) 433-7300
www.americanairlines.com

ASA
(800) 325-1999

British Airways
(800) 247-9297

(Airlines, continued)

Delta
(800) 221-1212
www.delta-air.com

Frontier
(800) 432-1359
www.frontierairlines.com

Hooters Air
(888) 359-4668

Hawaiian
(866) 367-5320
www.hawaiianair.com

Korean Air
(800) 438-5000

Northwest
(800) 225-2525
www.nwa.com

Southwest
(800) 435-9792
www.southwest.com

TWA
(800) 221-2000
www.twa.com

United
(800) 241-6522
www.united.com

US Airways
(800) 428-4322
www.usairways.com

How to Get to the Airport

Odds are, your roommate will be from the greater Atlanta area, so you can always bum a ride with him or her if you need to get to the airport. Otherwise, a cab ride to the airport costs $90.

AAA Airport Express
(404) 767-2000

$30 per person each way. Group rates available.

(Get to the Airport, continued)

Atlanta Arrangements
(404) 443-5959

Vans or minibuses available for 10–22 people. $250–$350.

Daytime Transportation Inc.
(770) 939-2337

Transportation for groups of 10–15.

Greyhound

220 W Broad St.
(706) 549-2255
(800) 231-2222
www.greyhound.com

Travel Agents

Adventures in the Realm LTD
1576 Cleveland Rd.
(706) 548-7642

All Aboard Travel and Meeting Planning Services
297 Prince Ave.
(706) 354-6909

Global Escapes, Inc.
697 Milledge Ave.
(706) 549-1164

The Joy of Travel
1307 Cleveland Rd.
(706) 552-3300

Orbit Travel Agency
(706) 549-7009
www.orbit-travel.com

Students Speak Out On...
Transportation

{ **"Public transportation is pretty convenient. There's the Athens city bus, which is free as long as you have your student ID. There are taxis. Also, there are the University buses, which take you all over campus."**

Q "**There is a city bus system that runs all around Athens, and it's really convenient**. It runs past almost every apartment complex in the city. There's also the UGA bus system that runs on campus. Campus is so big that you need to ride a bus to get from one end to the other. You could walk, as I've done many times, but that takes about 20 minutes."

Q "Public **transportation is pretty reliable**, so long as you know which bus goes where. We also have a wonderful campus bus line that takes you anywhere that you want to go on campus. There is a requirement of knowing which bus goes where, but the school also supplies bus schedules, and they are on each of the buses. The University system provides a map with all of the different bus routes marked on it, and I'm sure that the Athens transit system does the same thing."

Q "Public transportation doesn't exist in the South. **There is a crappy bus line in Athens**, and that is it."

Q "I took 'the Bus' one semester, and I'll never do that again. It was hot, and it gave me a headache every morning. **Parking is expensive**, but after that experience, I think it's worth it."

Q "We have two bus lines in Athens: one is the University bus system, and the other is the city's bus transit system. 'the Bus' (city transit) also runs through campus with the University buses. **The bus goes to most apartment complexes off campus** so that students can take a bus from their apartments to campus."

Q "**Public transportation is great here**. On campus, the bus will take you anywhere you want to go, although they are usually a bit crowded. There are also city buses that come from many apartment complexes, so students can get to campus."

Q "**The UGA buses are huge, but they're always packed**. I think they need more Milledge Avenue buses running, because those are always the most crowded. Sometimes, they forget to turn the air on in the buses, and that is horrible when it's hot and humid outside."

Q "The Athens Transit Bus system runs routes just about everywhere in the town. Some routes are placed throughout areas of off-campus apartments, which are **very convenient and free for students**."

Q "The **UGA buses are usually crowded**, and sometimes really hot, but they're much better than walking from one end of campus to another."

Q "The **Athens buses that come onto campus are packed** by the time they start toward apartment complexes. I would hate to do that every day, because I'm sure that's at least a 15-minute ride."

Q "I've taken every UGA bus on campus, and **I think they're a great way to move students fast**, and the campus is too big for some people to make it to classes on time."

Q "The buses give me a headache, and the ones with the vinyl seat covers make me slip and slide all over the place every time the bus makes a turn. **If you get a driver who is mad at the world, as some of them are, you may become nauseated real fast**."

The College Prowler Take On...
Transportation

The UGA buses run quite efficiently, and are a great way to get around our sprawling campus. Students who don't have a parking permit can take the Athens Transit buses to and from campus. If you don't have a car here, try to bum rides off your friends. The buses usually require a long wait, and it's just a bad situation for all students when it's hot and crowded, and it seems as if everyone has had a long day. The cabs here can be a little pricey, and even a bit shady, but if you need a ride home from someone who is slightly less buzzed than you, then our cabbies will do just fine.

Having Hartsfield Airport an hour and a half away is convenient for out-of-staters, anyone going abroad, or on spring break trips. Students routinely find departing flights to just about any destination from Atlanta. Getting to the airport is not really complicated. Students are almost guaranteed to meet someone from Atlanta at UGA. It would be nearly impossible not to. Try to get a ride with these people to the airport.

The College Prowler® Grade on

Transportation: C

A high grade for Transportation indicates that campus buses, public buses, cabs, and rental cars are readily-available and affordable. Other determining factors include proximity to an airport and the necessity of transportation.

Weather

The Lowdown On...
Weather

Average Temperature:

Fall:	60°F
Winter:	43°F
Spring:	62°F
Summer:	80°F

Average Precipitation:

Fall:	3.32 in.
Winter:	4.19 in.
Spring:	4.60 in.
Summer:	4.17 in.

Students Speak Out On...
Weather

> "The weather is beautiful. I've never seen skies as blue as the skies over Athens. It's a really beautiful place, nestled in the North Georgia Mountains. I love it here, and it has a very nice climate."

Q "The **weather is hot and humid in the summer**; pretty chilly at night in the fall; cold, but not frigid, during the winter; and beautiful during the spring. You will have to bring a whole range of clothing to school!"

Q "The winters are very mild. It never really gets cold, for the most part. However, the drawback is that the summers are scorching. **The 98-degree heat wouldn't be so bad in July if the humidity level wasn't 90 percent**. I won't lie to you and say that the summers are tame. They most certainly aren't."

Q "It can be **miserably hot in the summer in Athens**. The rest of the year is pretty nice, and the winters are mild."

Q "**The weather is wonderful**! That's one of the main reasons I came to the South to go to school. It's so nice being in Georgia. It can get hot, but it's usually not uncomfortably hot. During the winter, there is very rarely snow, and, most of the time, I don't even have to wear a heavy coat. The spring is exceptionally beautiful. There are flowering trees everywhere, and the whole campus turns green—it's gorgeous."

Q "You get **the best of all four seasons here**. I really love fall and spring in Athens."

Q "I guess as someone who has lived in Georgia all his life, I don't really have a lot of other places that I can compare it to, but in comparison it to places that I've visited, **the weather is pretty moderate**. It never gets particularly cold, but it does get too hot for some people's taste (it can get up into the 90s during the summer). Overall, the weather is great. It's the reason a lot of Northerners move down here."

Q "**The weather here is amazing**. I came from Pennsylvania, and this is a drastic change. We have warm falls and springs, and winter doesn't get too cold, either. I love the weather down here."

Q "The weather in Athens is usually falls into the 'hot' to 'stifling hot' category, but **the winters are nice, cool, and sometimes cold**. It rarely snows here, but it is cold enough to wear coats sometimes."

Q "**Late spring through early fall is very hot**. Plenty of shorts and T-shirts are highly recommended. Coats and sweaters are a good idea for the winter, but it rarely ever snows here."

Q "I have literally changed my clothes four times a day for weeks on end because **the weather in Athens can be so unpredictable**. It will be cold in the morning, scorching in the afternoon, rainy around dinner, and then cool again at night."

Q "People not from the South need to note that when you hear that it's hot in Georgia, it's not the kind of hot they're used to. **The air is thick and humid—you will sweat just walking out to your car**. It makes you not want to do anything but drink water and go swimming, and sometimes it's even too hot to do that."

The College Prowler Take On...
Weather

When school starts in the fall, it is extremely warm outside, and the humidity is in full effect. Walking to class in the middle of the day is a guaranteed way to get nice and sweaty, especially with a big heavy backpack over your shoulders. Everything is really green, though, and the evenings are cool and breezy. Once October rolls around, it gets a little cooler, and it's usually sunny, making for great football weather. The leaves are beautiful as they change colors in the fall. The temperature fluctuates a lot—one minute it will be chilly, the next you'll be toweling the sweat off of your forehead with a bandana.

The heaviest clothes you'll need for fall are a good sweatshirt or sweater and a pair of jeans. Winter comes to Athens sometime in November and lasts through February. Winters are generally mild, but you will need a coat of some sort. Whatever you do, don't forget an umbrella. There are a good number of bleak, rainy, sunless days, but winter does not last for long, so it's tolerable. Spring is amazing in Athens, as it is all over the South, but it is a tricky time for dressing appropriately, as it is often cool in the mornings and evenings but very hot in the middle of the day. It rains often in the springtime, sometimes it's a light sprinkle, other times it's a torrential downpour. When summer comes back around in May, the heat and humidity settle in again. It also tends to rain hard for extended periods in the summer. Umbrellas are key because it's definitely too hot for a raincoat.

B+

The College Prowler® Grade on
Weather: B+

A high Weather grade designates that temperatures are mild and rarely reach extremes, that the campus tends to be sunny rather than rainy, and that weather is fairly consistent rather than unpredictable.

Report Card Summary

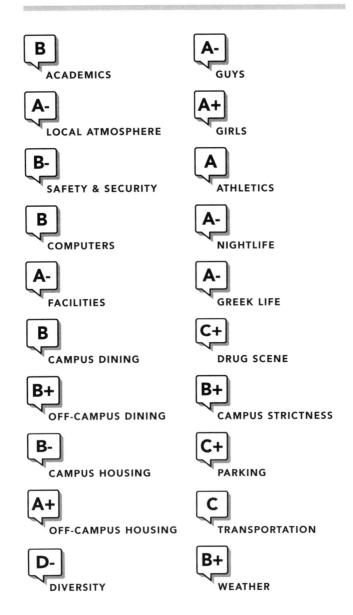

B
ACADEMICS

A-
GUYS

A-
LOCAL ATMOSPHERE

A+
GIRLS

B-
SAFETY & SECURITY

A
ATHLETICS

B
COMPUTERS

A-
NIGHTLIFE

A-
FACILITIES

A-
GREEK LIFE

B
CAMPUS DINING

C+
DRUG SCENE

B+
OFF-CAMPUS DINING

B+
CAMPUS STRICTNESS

B-
CAMPUS HOUSING

C+
PARKING

A+
OFF-CAMPUS HOUSING

C
TRANSPORTATION

D-
DIVERSITY

B+
WEATHER

Overall Experience

Students Speak Out On...
Overall Experience

{ **"I would not trade my time at UGA for anything in the world. I can't imagine myself at any other university. Most people who go to school here can't either."**

Q **"UGA is great, and I love it.** Sometimes I wish that I had chosen a smaller school, but overall, I am happy that I am here. After my first year, I realized that this was a really big school and found myself feeling more and more like a number rather than an actual student. I had a great time and love this school, but I think that you should consider the size in making your decision."

Q "Athens and UGA are like drugs; you get addicted to them. **People love it so much when they're here.** It's great. I can't say enough about it."

Q "I had the choice of going to a small private college, and I am so glad that I chose UGA instead. **The trick to succeeding at a big university is to find your niche**. I suggest getting involved. Whether it's in a Greek society or in any of our hundreds of student organizations, you can meet people with similar beliefs and interests while also being exposed to tons others!"

Q "I absolutely love UGA! If I had the opportunity to go back and do it all over again, I wouldn't change a thing. I have enjoyed my stay here, and I can't wait for the new semester to begin. **Athens is pretty quiet in the summer, but it's pretty rocking in the fall and spring**. I would never go to another college. UGA has more than met my expectations. It gets better and better as each day goes by."

Q "I wouldn't attend college at any other university. **UGA simply has everything**. I know that I sound like a salesman pitching the school, but I have simply loved my three years at UGA, and it wasn't even my first choice for college. The size of the school takes a little getting used to, but now it feels like my home."

Q "Everyone that I know loves UGA! **You get out of it what you want to get out of it**. You will make so many friends living in your dorm, and you will love it. I transferred here, so I didn't get to live in a dorm here, but I did at Southern, so I didn't miss out on that experience. But UGA is really fun. Sometimes a little too much fun, but overall, it's great!"

Q "My overall experience has been amazing. I love it here, and I am so glad I came. I have had so much fun these past few years, while also getting a great education. In town, **there is always something going on**, and there are always a ton of people around. It just makes for a great college experience. I wouldn't trade my experience for anything in the world."

Q "I love this school. I am so happy I decided to come here, and **I know once I leave I will be jealous of every freshman** who is standing at the beginning of what will most definitely be the best four years of their lives."

Q "I love UGA. I have met so many great people and **once you figure out the campus, it doesn't seem so big**. I do not wish to be at any other school."

Q "I really don't think you could find a single person here who doesn't like being at UGA. **This place has treated me very well, and I'll be sad to leave**."

Q "I transferred here, so I experienced a lot of roadblocks originally in registering, getting an apartment, and making friends, but I like it a lot now. The people are really friendly, and **you can take all kinds of interesting classes in all different fields**."

Q "I can't even put into words my overall experience here. I would tell anyone looking for a college to come here. **UGA has been one of the best experiences of my whole life**, and I have a feeling that 20 years from now, it will still probably be true."

Q "UGA is a lot like a big family. There are people that annoy you, and people you don't want to see, but overall, **you have an overwhelming fondness for people** because you know you are all sharing something in common that you can be proud of."

The College Prowler Take On...
Overall Experience

One of the most amazing things about students at UGA is that I have never heard one person say they don't like being here. UGA and Athens have so much to offer in so many different categories, that there really is something for everyone. The positive energy of 30,000 people who are happy to be here is captivating, and something you will instantly want to be a part of. It will not take long before you regard Athens as your second home, and after about a week, most students forget how big a school it is.

It's exciting to be in Athens because there is always something going on, whether it is entertainment, a demonstration, job fairs, or just a chance to hang out with people you just met who are now your best friends. Students are encouraged to explore their talents and make the most of their four years here, and most students are able to achieve their ultimate "college experience." Sometimes, it seems like we are all characters in some cheesy teen movie because college life in Athens is so classic, but academically, socially, and personally, this school seems to have changed most of us for the better.

The Inside Scoop

The Lowdown On...
The Inside Scoop

UGA Slang:

Know the slang, know the school. The following is a list of things you really need to know before coming to UGA. The more of these words you know, the better off you'll be.

Ag Hill, East Campus Express, East-West, Milledge Avenue, North-South, Orbit, Russell Hall – Names of UGA buses that run all over campus.

The Arch – The symbol of UGA is a three-pillar arch that stands at the north end of campus facing Broad Street. The pillars stand for wisdom, justice, and moderation.

"Between the Hedges" – Refers to our football field at Sanford Stadium. There are hedges on either side of the field so games are played "between the hedges."

→

College – There are colleges within the University of Georgia that specialize in one area of expertise, for example, there is the Grady College of Journalism and the Terry College of Business. The term "college" does not mean the school as a whole.

G-Day – The day in the spring when the football team holds a scrimmage game.

Hairy Dawg – A sort of unofficial mascot, usually at basketball and football games. He is in a costume, as opposed to Uga, who is really a bulldog . . . we think.)

MyID – This is the first part of your UGA Mail account. (whatever is before "@uga.edu.")

North Campus – Refers to the oldest section of UGA, home to many administration buildings now.

OASIS – "Online Access to Student Information Systems." This is the online program, through which students register for classes, keep track of their accounts, calculate their own GPA, and other functions.

O-House – Refers to both Oglethorpe House dorm, and Oglethorpe Dining Commons, so be careful.

P-J – Refers to the psychology and journalism buildings located on the corner of Sanford Drive and Baldwin Street.

Ramsey – Ramsey Center for Physical Fitness.

Snelling, Bolton – Dining halls on campus.

Tate – Refers to the Tate Student Center.

Uga – Our beloved bulldog mascot.

Things I Wish I Knew Before Coming to UGA

- Try to have a major in mind before you get here.
- Central air means nothing. Invest in a fan.
- Get the seven-day meal plan.
- Don't bother bringing sweaters until after Thanksgiving.
- You are not guaranteed access to your first-choice major.
- You're going to want a camera.
- Stock up on red and black clothes.
- Just because there's no attendance policy doesn't mean you should skip class.
- Just because you started class at 8 a.m. in high school does not mean you should do so in college.
- If you don't like football, this may not be the best place for you, and you will probably get fed up fast.

Tips to Succeed at UGA

- Take fun electives; there's a lot of unique classes available.
- Research potential professors before choosing your classes— some are much easier than others who are teaching the same courses.
- Go to class!
- Don't ever fall behind in reading.
- Make use of all the facilities at Ramsey. You won't get equipment like this for free anywhere else.
- Do your own homework.
- Don't waste your time trying to study in the dorms. Head to the library or the SLC.
- Always dispute bad grades—you may even be given a second chance.
- Go out on the weekend. Go to shows, plays, concerts, games, protests, anything you might not get a chance to do again.

School Spirit

School spirit is strong at the University of Georgia. Alumni support, both financially and physically, at University events is overwhelming. Students and alumni join together for many University fundraisers and causes. Football games unite thousands of students and fans that might have nothing else in common but a love for the school and the Dawgs.

The pursuit of excellence within the University is a challenge undertaken by students and alumni from all walks of life. Most people affiliated with UGA want it to remain great. Students and alumni are proud of their UGA education, and proud to be a part of a school with so much character. Students, faculty, and alumni are very involved in the affairs of the University's administration, and the *Red and Black* newspaper keeps everyone informed as to what is going on.

Dawgs fans have been through a lot, both good and bad, but they remain dedicated and unwavering. Loyalty is key to being a Dawg. The fans here are great, and easily some of the best in the nation. They are always supportive, always faithful, and definitely know how to have a good time.

Traditions

Bulldogs

The term "Georgia Bulldogs" came from an article written in 1920. First it was a nickname, believed to pay tribute to Yale University where our first president, Abraham Baldwin, attended college. On November 3, 1920, Morgan Blake of the *Atlanta Journal* wrote, "The Georgia Bulldog would sound good because there is a certain dignity about a bulldog, as well as ferocity." Three days later, on November 6, 1920, after a UGA football game, Cliff Wheatley used the name "Bulldogs" five times in his story, and we've been known as the Bulldogs ever since.

Uga

Voted the best mascot in the country by *Sports Illustrated*, Uga comes from a long line of bulldogs owned by Frank W. "Sonny" Sieler of Savannah, GA. The current line began with Uga I, a solid white English Bulldog, the grandson of a former Georgia mascot. The most famous Uga was Uga V, who actually appeared in the movie "Midnight in the Garden of Good and Evil." He also posed for the cover of *Sports Illustrated* when he was named the best mascot in the nation. We are now up to Uga VI. All the Uga's lived in Savannah, and travel to Athens for football games.

The Georgia "G"

The Georgia "G" was originally designed by head football coach Vince Dooley in 1964. Dooley liked the look of the "G" on helmets worn by the Green Bay Packers, and designed Georgia's "G" accordingly, though utilizing a different color scheme. The design features a black oval "G" surrounded by a white oval background. A white stripe encircles the "G" over the top. A smaller black stripe was added inside the white stripe over the top in 1996 by new head football coach Jim Donnan.

The Chapel Bell

Georgia fans ring the chapel bell after a Georgia football victory. This tradition began in the 1890s, and used to be a chore reserved for freshmen. Now, however, students and alumni eagerly rush to the Chapel after a football victory for a chance to ring the chapel bell. At orientation, incoming freshmen get to ring the bell.

"Glory, Glory"

One of UGA's oldest traditions is the singing of our school fight song, "Glory, Glory," which is sung to the tune of "The Battle Hymn of the Republic." Depending on our opponent, improvisations in the last line of the song may resound from the stands. The line is supposed to go "G-E-O-R-G-I-A," but sometimes becomes "And to hell with Flo-ri-da," or something along those lines.

"How 'Bout Them Dogs"

This line has become the battle cry of Dawg fans. It is believed to have originated in the 1970s and gained momentum when a major wire service picked it up after Georgia beat Notre Dame in the Sugar Bowl and claimed the national championship. Many newspapers thereafter used it as a headline.

Landmarks

The Hedges

The hedges in Sanford Stadium have been standing proudly since its dedication in 1929. "Between the hedges" is a phrase supposedly originating from Atlanta writer Grantland Rice when he said of an upcoming game, "that the Bulldogs will have their opponent 'between the hedges.'"

The Arch

The arch is located at the edge of North Campus, facing downtown Athens. It was installed in 1864, and remains today. The Arch is also the official emblem of the University of Georgia, appearing on official documents and Georgia merchandise. Originally, freshmen were forbidden to walk under the arch. Nowadays, anyone can walk under it, but there are mythical consequences. Supposedly, any undergraduate who walks under the Arch will not graduate and will become infertile. You will see most people choosing to walk around the Arch if you watch closely.

Homecoming

Every year before Homecoming, numerous student groups sneak out to Sanford Drive late at night and paint their group's homecoming theme on the street in front of Sanford Stadium. The designs are always bright and bold, and last for months afterwards. There is also a big homecoming parade downtown during Homecoming week. Students and locals always flock to catch candy and see the floats. Onlookers can also get a glimpse of everyone's favorite bulldog, Uga.

Finding a Job or Internship

The Lowdown On...
Finding a Job or Internship

Career Center:
UGA Career Center
Clark Howell Hall
(706) 542-3375
(706) 542-8431 (fax)
career@uga.edu
Hours: Monday–Friday
8 a.m.–5 p.m.

Services Available:
• Assistance in job searches
• Career counseling
• Choosing a major
• Employer relations skills
• Experiential education
• Graduate and professional school preparation
• Resume and interview workshops
• Skill training

Firms that Most Frequently Hire Graduates

Accenture, Advantage Behavioral Health, American International Group, The BellSouth Corporation, Chick-fil-A, Deloitte & Touche, Emory University, Ernst & Young, Ferguson Enterprises, Hewitt Associates, KPMG, Liberty Mutual, Philip Morris USA, Pricewaterhouse Coopers, Progressive Insurance, Publix, Pulte Homes, State of Georgia, SunTrust, University of Georgia, UPS, USDA, Walgreens, Wal-Mart, and Zurcih North America

Advice

The first person to consult about a job or internship is your academic adviser. He or she can keep you informed of opportunities in your particular field of interest, as your advisor's domain is within your designated college. He or she should be able to make the necessary job connections for you, as many colleges have lists of internships ready for the taking. If you are not satisfied, however, you can always try the Career Center on campus for help in a broader sense, or to work on career-related skills.

Average Salary Information

The following statistics represent average annual starting salaries for UGA graduates from each college.

College Average Salary

College	Average Salary
Agricultural and Environmental Sciences	$32,000
Arts and Sciences	$30,000
Business	$35,000
Education	$32,000
Environment and Design	$32,000
Family and Consumer Sciences	$27,000
Journalism and Mass Communication	$28,000
Social Work	$26,000

Alumni

The Lowdown On...
Alumni

Office:

UGA Alumni Relations
Wray-Nicholson House
298 S Hull St.
(706) 542-2251
(800) 606-8786
www.alumni.uga.edu/alumni

UGA Alumni Association

Atlanta Alumni Center,
Atlanta Financial Center

3333 Peachtree Rd. NE
South Tower, Suite 210
Atlanta

(404) 266-2622

Services Available

The UGA Alumni Association provides graduates with financial services, national discounts, and keeps members informed of special University events. Additionally, it serves as a forum for alumni to maintain relationships with current fellow students and professors.

Major Alumni Events

Alumni Tours Abroad, First Friday Pep Rally, SEC Alumni Fall Kickoff, UGA Alumni Night

Alumni Publications

Around the Arch

The Georgia Bulldog

Georgia Magazine

Did You Know?

Famous UGA Alumni

Anne Barge – Famous bridal gown designer

Chris Carter – Army Captain (on the news in 2003, waving UGA flag in front of Saddam Hussein's presidential palace in Baghdad)

Neill Slaughter – Famous artist

Dominique Wilkins – Future NBA Hall of Famer

Student Organizations

Student Associations

Here is a sampling of UGA's student organizations. For the complete list, visit *www.uga.edu/stuact/studentorganizations/adguide.pdf*

Ad Club – *www.uga.edu/adclub*
African Student Union – *www.uga.edu/~asu*
American Society of Interior Design
Ceramic Student Organization – *www.tsaupe@uga.edu*
College Republicans – *www.ugarepublicans.com*
Graduate Minority Business Association – *www.uga.edu/gmba*
Guitarists' Guild
Habitat for Humanity – *www.uga.edu/habitat*
Hillel – Campus Center for Jewish Life – *www.uga.edu/hillel*
Hispanic Student Association – *www.uga.edu/hsa*
Horticulture Club – *www.uga.edu/hort/hortclub.html*
Hype-HIV/AIDS Youth Prevention – *www.aidscoalitionnega.org*
In-Line Roller Hockey Club
Institute of Biological Engineering – *www.engr.uga.edu/resources/clubs/ibe*
Insurance Society – *www.terry.uga.edu/insurance*
International Business

Japan Club – *www.uga.edu/jac*

Karate Club – *www.uga.edu/~tkd*

Kayak Club

Law Partners of the UGA School of Law

Leadership Resource Team – *www.uga.edu/stuact/leadership/ leaderhome.html*

Libertarians of UGA – *www.uga.edu/libertarians*

Music Therapy Club

Muslim Student Association

Minority Pre-Medical Student Association

Paintball Club

Pamoja Dance Company – *www.uga.edu/aacc/pamoja.htm*

Poultry Science Club

Safe Campus Now – *www.uga.edu/~safe-campus/*

Society of Consumer Affairs Professionals

Social Work Club – *www.ssw.uga.edu*

Students for the American Red Cross

Society of Professional Journalists – *www.uga.edu/spj*

Swing Club

UGA Ice Hockey – www.ugahockey.com

University Union – *www.union.uga.edu*

Undergraduate Mock Trial Association

University Round Table – *www.uga.edu/urt*

Wildlife Society – *www.forestry.uga.edu/warnell/tws/index.html*

Young Democrats – *www.uga.edu/yngdems*

Young Life

The Best & Worst

The Ten **BEST** Things About UGA

1	The people
2	Football season
3	Downtown
4	The weather
5	Uga
6	The music scene
7	Proximity to Atlanta
8	The food
9	The parties
10	Ramsey

The Ten WORST Things About UGA

1 Constant construction

2 Competition for majors

3 Humidity

4 Diversity

5 Greedy and/or stupid athletes and coaches

6 Parking

7 Teachers you can't understand

8 Administration politics

9 Annual tuition increases they try to sneak up on you

10 As soon as you think you're starting to look pretty good, you'll run across someone that looks like a Hawaiian Tropic model . . . and your self-esteem plummets.

Visiting

The Lowdown On...
Visiting

Hotel Information:

Best Western Colonial Inn
170 N Milledge Ave.
(706) 546-7311
Distance from Campus: 1 mile
Price Range: $60–$65

Comfort Inn
3980 Atlanta Hwy.
(706) 227-9700
Distance from Campus: 5 miles
Price Range: $70–$75

Courtyard by Marriott
166 Finley St.
(706) 369-7000
Distance from Campus: 1 mile
Price Range: $60–$65

Foundry Park Inn and Spa
295 E Dougherty St.
(706) 549-7020
Distance from Campus: 1 mile
Price Range: $90–$95

Hampton Inn
2220 W Broad St.
(706) 548-9600
Distance from Campus: 1 mile
Price Range: $60–$65

Holiday Inn
197 E Broad St.
(706) 549-4433
Distance from Campus: 1 mile
Price Range: $80–$85

Suburban Extended Stay Hotel
2044 S Milledge Dr.
(706) 208-8812

(Suburban, continued)
Distance from Campus: 4 miles
Price Range: $50–$60

Travelodge Inn Downtown
898 W Broad Street
(706) 549-5400
Distance from Campus: 1 mile
Price Range: $50–$55

The UGA Center for Continuing Education
1197 S Lumpkin St.
(800) 488-7827
Distance from Campus: 0 miles
Price Range: $80–$85

Take a Campus Virtual Tour

www.uga.edu/virtualtour

Campus Tours

The Visitors Center conducts campus tours every day of the week, with three tours each weekday, two on Saturday, and one on Sunday. Each tour begins on a mini-bus and participants will receive an hour-long driving and walking tour of campus. Reservations are a must as space is limited on the bus. Weekends, teacher workdays, and spring-break dates fill up fast. A self-guided tour offers the same tour route used on student-led tours. You can stop by the Visitors Center and pick up a copy. The Visitors Center also provides a 30-minute audio tour of North Campus. Cassettes and walkmans can be checked out at the Visitors Center.

The Visitors Center offers special tours for various groups including school groups, campus groups, and alumni and community groups. Special tours can be scheduled by calling the Visitors Center manager.

For more information or to make reservations, call (706) 542-0842.

Directions to Campus

Driving from the North

- Take 441 South from Commerce, Georgia.

- Travel underneath the Athens Perimeter (Loop 10) and then make an immediate left onto it.

- Continue on Athens Perimeter following signs for the GA Loop 10 (you will need to exit to stay on the loop) until you reach the College Station Road exit (exit #14).

- Exit at College Station Road and make a right.

- Go through one light, and the Visitor's Center will be on the right in the Four Towers Building. Parking is available in front of the Visitors Center.

Driving from the South

- Take US 129/441 or GA 15 North into Watkinsville.

- In Watkinsville, Hwy.15 and US 129 meet up. Go North toward Athens.

- As you near Athens, there will be a sign signaling Hwy. 441 North, and a right turn. (There will also be a sign for the University of Georgia.) Turn right at this sign onto Loop 10.

- Continue on Loop 10 until you reach exit 14, the College Station Road exit.

- Exit off Loop 10 and turn left onto College Station Road.

- After going under the bypass, go through two lights, and just after the second one, the Visitors Center will be on your right. It is located in the Four Towers Building.

Driving from the East

- Take US 78 West to Athens.

- In Athens, travel under the GA Loop 10, and then take a left at the next traffic light, going westbound.

- Exit Loop 10 at the College Station Road exit (#14), turn right onto College Station Road and continue through one light. The Visitors Center will be on your right in the Four Towers Building.

Words to Know

Academic Probation – A suspension imposed on a student if he or she fails to keep up with the school's minimum academic requirements. Those unable to improve their grades after receiving this warning can face dismissal.

Beer Pong/Beirut – A drinking game involving cups of beer arranged in a pyramid shape on each side of a table. The goal is to get a ping pong ball into one of the opponent's cups by throwing the ball or hitting it with a paddle. If the ball lands in a cup, the opponent is required to drink the beer.

Bid – An invitation from a fraternity or sorority to 'pledge' (join) that specific house.

Blue-Light Phone – Brightly-colored phone posts with a blue light bulb on top. These phones exist for security purposes and are located at various outside locations around most campuses. In an emergency, a student can pick up one of these phones (free of charge) to connect with campus police or a security escort.

Campus Police – Police who are specifically assigned to a given institution. Campus police are typically not regular city officers; they are employed by the university in a full-time capacity.

Club Sports – A level of sports that falls somewhere between varsity and intramural. If a student is unable to commit to a varsity team but has a lot of passion for athletics, a club sport could be a better, less intense option. Even less demanding, intramural (IM) sports often involve no traveling and considerably less time.

Cocaine – An illegal drug. Also known as "coke" or "blow," cocaine often resembles a white crystalline or powdery substance. It is highly addictive and dangerous.

Common Application – An application with which students can apply to multiple schools.

Course Registration – The period of official class selection for the upcoming quarter or semester. Prior to registration, it is best to prepare several back-up courses in case a particular class becomes full. If a course is full, students can place themselves on the waitlist, although this still does not guarantee entry.

Division Athletics – Athletic classifications range from Division I to Division III. Division IA is the most competitive, while Division III is considered to be the least competitive.

Dorm – A dorm (or dormitory) is an on-campus housing facility. Dorms can provide a range of options from suite-style rooms to more communal options that include shared bathrooms. Most first-year students live in dorms. Some upperclassmen who wish to stay on campus also choose this option.

Early Action – An application option with which a student can apply to a school and receive an early acceptance response without a binding commitment. This system is becoming less and less available.

Early Decision – An application option that students should use only if they are certain they plan to attend the school in question. If a student applies using the early decision option and is admitted, he or she is required and bound to attend that university. Admission rates are usually higher among students who apply through early decision, as the student is clearly indicating that the school is his or her first choice.

Ecstasy – An illegal drug. Also known as "E" or "X," ecstasy looks like a pill and most resembles an aspirin. Considered a party drug, ecstasy is very dangerous and can be deadly.

Ethernet – An extremely fast Internet connection available in most university-owned residence halls. To use an Ethernet connection properly, a student will need a network card and cable for his or her computer.

Fake ID – A counterfeit identification card that contains false information. Most commonly, students get fake IDs with altered birthdates so that they appear to be older than 21 (and therefore of legal drinking age). Even though it is illegal, many college students have fake IDs in hopes of purchasing alcohol or getting into bars.

Frosh – Slang for "freshman" or "freshmen."

Hazing – Initiation rituals administered by some fraternities or sororities as part of the pledging process. Many universities have outlawed hazing due to its degrading, and sometimes dangerous, nature.

Intramurals (IMs) – A popular, and usually free, sport league in which students create teams and compete against one another. These sports vary in competitiveness and can include a range of activities—everything from billiards to water polo. IM sports are a great way to meet people with similar interests.

Keg – Officially called a half-barrel, a keg contains roughly 200 12-ounce servings of beer.

LSD – An illegal drug, also known as acid, this hallucinogenic drug most commonly resembles a tab of paper.

Marijuana – An illegal drug, also known as weed or pot; along with alcohol, marijuana is one of the most commonly-found drugs on campuses across the country.

Major –The focal point of a student's college studies; a specific topic that is studied for a degree. Examples of majors include physics, English, history, computer science, economics, business, and music. Many students decide on a specific major before arriving on campus, while others are simply "undecided" until declaring a major. Those who are extremely interested in two areas can also choose to double major.

Meal Block – The equivalent of one meal. Students on a meal plan usually receive a fixed number of meals per week. Each meal, or "block," can be redeemed at the school's dining facilities in place of cash. Often, a student's weekly allotment of meal blocks will be forfeited if not used.

Minor – An additional focal point in a student's education. Often serving as a complement or addition to a student's main area of focus, a minor has fewer requirements and prerequisites to fulfill than a major. Minors are not required for graduation from most schools; however some students who want to explore many different interests choose to pursue both a major and a minor.

Mushrooms – An illegal drug. Also known as "'shrooms," this drug resembles regular mushrooms but is extremely hallucinogenic.

Off-Campus Housing – Housing from a particular landlord or rental group that is not affiliated with the university. Depending on the college, off-campus housing can range from extremely popular to non-existent. Students who choose to live off campus are typically given more freedom, but they also have to deal with possible subletting scenarios, furniture, bills, and other issues. In addition to these factors, rental prices and distance often affect a student's decision to move off campus.

Office Hours – Time that teachers set aside for students who have questions about coursework. Office hours are a good forum for students to go over any problems and to show interest in the subject material.

Pledging – The early phase of joining a fraternity or sorority, pledging takes place after a student has gone through rush and received a bid. Pledging usually lasts between one and two semesters. Once the pledging period is complete and a particular student has done everything that is required to become a member, that student is considered a brother or sister. If a fraternity or a sorority would decide to "haze" a group of students, this initiation would take place during the pledging period.

Private Institution – A school that does not use tax revenue to subsidize education costs. Private schools typically cost more than public schools and are usually smaller.

Prof – Slang for "professor."

Public Institution – A school that uses tax revenue to subsidize education costs. Public schools are often a good value for in-state residents and tend to be larger than most private colleges.

Quarter System (or Trimester System) – A type of academic calendar system. In this setup, students take classes for three academic periods. The first quarter usually starts in late September or early October and concludes right before Christmas. The second quarter usually starts around early to mid–January and finishes up around March or April. The last academic quarter, or "third quarter," usually starts in late March or early April and finishes up in late May or Mid-June. The fourth quarter is summer. The major difference between the quarter system and semester system is that students take more, less comprehensive courses under the quarter calendar.

RA (Resident Assistant) – A student leader who is assigned to a particular floor in a dormitory in order to help to the other students who live there. An RA's duties include ensuring student safety and providing assistance wherever possible.

Recitation – An extension of a specific course; a review session. Some classes, particularly large lectures, are supplemented with mandatory recitation sessions that provide a relatively personal class setting.

Rolling Admissions – A form of admissions. Most commonly found at public institutions, schools with this type of policy continue to accept students throughout the year until their class sizes are met. For example, some schools begin accepting students as early as December and will continue to do so until April or May.

Room and Board – This figure is typically the combined cost of a university-owned room and a meal plan.

Room Draw/Housing Lottery – A common way to pick on-campus room assignments for the following year. If a student decides to remain in university-owned housing, he or she is assigned a unique number that, along with seniority, is used to determine his or her housing for the next year.

Rush – The period in which students can meet the brothers and sisters of a particular chapter and find out if a given fraternity or sorority is right for them. Rushing a fraternity or a sorority is not a requirement at any school. The goal of rush is to give students who are serious about pledging a feel for what to expect.

Semester System – The most common type of academic calendar system at college campuses. This setup typically includes two semesters in a given school year. The fall semester starts around the end of August or early September and concludes before winter vacation. The spring semester usually starts in mid-January and ends in late April or May.

Student Center/Rec Center/Student Union – A common area on campus that often contains study areas, recreation facilities, and eateries. This building is often a good place to meet up with fellow students; depending on the school, the student center can have a huge role or a non-existent role in campus life.

Student ID – A university-issued photo ID that serves as a student's key to school-related functions. Some schools require students to show these cards in order to get into dorms, libraries, cafeterias, and other facilities. In addition to storing meal plan information, in some cases, a student ID can actually work as a debit card and allow students to purchase things from bookstores or local shops.

Suite – A type of dorm room. Unlike dorms that feature communal bathrooms shared by the entire floor, suites offer bathrooms shared only among the suite. Suite-style dorm rooms can house anywhere from two to ten students.

TA (Teacher's Assistant) – An undergraduate or grad student who helps in some manner with a specific course. In some cases, a TA will teach a class, assist a professor, grade assignments, or conduct office hours.

Undergraduate – A student in the process of studying for his or her bachelor's degree.

ABOUT THE AUTHOR

Writing this book was a great way for me to collect everything I want to remember from my experience at UGA, and condense it down to create my own little scrapbook. It has allowed me to gain writing experience, and has shaped my career goals in the process. I am hoping to continue writing, in all its forms, throughout my career. I am currently a rising senior at the University of Georgia, and a Consumer Journalism major with an emphasis in Fashion Merchandising and Advertising. The thing I love about writing for advertising is the search for human truths, and little insights that you can convey to other people. Writing this book was much the same way. I hope it has offered some kind of insight into real life at UGA, so you can get an idea of what to expect, rather than vague, meaningless descriptions from a brochure.

I guess the best way to describe my college experience so far is to call it an adventure of sorts. I have made huge mistakes, gotten arrogant, and consequently been humbled. I have learned how to meet people, give presentations to groups of 300, and make decisions like an adult. I think college is a really important time for self-discovery, and I hope wherever you choose to go, you become more of the person you want to be as an adult.

I would like to thank all my homies who gave me quotes and tips for writing this book, and who were continually excited for its publication. You all are the biggest reason for my many great times. Also, I would like to thank everyone at College Prowler, especially Christina and Adam who have helped me out many times. Finally, I would like to dedicate this book to my mom, who will always be my biggest inspiration.

Nicole Goss
nicolegoss@collegeprowler.com

The College Prowler
Big Book of Colleges

Having Trouble Narrowing Down Your Choices?
Try Going Bigger!

BIG BOOK OF COLLEGES '09
7¼" X 10", 1248 Pages Paperback
$29.95 Retail
978-1-4274-0005-5

Choosing the perfect school can be an overwhelming challenge. Luckily, our *Big Book of Colleges* makes that task a little less daunting. We've packed it with overviews of our full library of single-school guides—more than 280 of the nation's top schools—giving you some much-needed perspective on your search.

College Prowler on the Web

Craving some electronic interaction? Check out the new and improved **CollegeProwler.com**! We've included the COMPLETE contents of more than 250 of our single-school guides on the Web—and you can gain access to all of them for just $39.95 per year!

Not only that, but non-subscribers can still view and compare our grades for each school, order books at our online bookstore, or enter our monthly scholarship contest. Don't get left in the dark when making your college decision. Let College Prowler be your guide!

Get the Jolt!

College Jolt gives you a peek behind the scenes

College Jolt is our new blog designed to hook you up with great information, funny videos, cool contests, awesome scholarship opportunities, and honest insight into who we are and what we're all about.

Check us out at ***www.collegejolt.com***

Need Help Paying For School?

Apply for our scholarship!

College Prowler awards thousands of dollars a year
to students who compose the best essays.
E-mail scholarship@collegeprowler.com for more
information, or call 1-800-290-2682.

Apply now at ***www.collegeprowler.com***

Tell Us What Life Is Really Like at Your School!

Have you ever wanted to let people know what your college is really like? Now's your chance to help millions of high school students choose the right college.

Let your voice be heard.

Check out *www.collegeprowler.com* for more info!

Need More Help?

Do you have more questions about this school? Can't find a certain statistic? College Prowler is here to help. We are the best source of college information out there. We have a network of thousands of students who can get the latest information on any school to you ASAP. E-mail us at info@collegeprowler.com with your college-related questions.

E-Mail Us Your College-Related Questions!

Check out *www.collegeprowler.com* for more details.
1-800-290-2682

Write For Us!

Get published! Voice your opinion.

Writing a College Prowler guidebook is both fun and rewarding; our open-ended format allows your own creativity free reign. Our writers have been featured in national newspapers and have seen their names in bookstores across the country. Now is your chance to break into the publishing industry with one of the country's fastest-growing publishers!

Apply now at ***www.collegeprowler.com***

Contact editor@collegeprowler.com or
call 1-800-290-2682 for more details.

Pros and Cons

Still can't figure out if this is the right school for you?
You've already read through this in-depth guide;
why not list the pros and cons? It will really help
with narrowing down your decision and determining
whether or not this school is right for you.

Pros	Cons
....	....
....	....
....	....
....	....
....	....
....	....
....	....
....	....
....	....
....	....
....	....
....	....
....	....

Pros and Cons

Still can't figure out if this is the right school for you?
You've already read through this in-depth guide;
why not list the pros and cons? It will really help
with narrowing down your decision and determining
whether or not this school is right for you.

Pros	Cons
....	....
....	....
....	....
....	....
....	....
....	....
....	....
....	....
....	....
....	....
....	....
....	....
....	....

Notes

....

....

....

....

....

....

....

....

....

....

....

....

....

Notes

....

....

....

....

....

....

....

....

....

....

....

....

....

Notes

....

....

....

....

....

....

....

....

....

....

....

....

....

Notes

....

....

....

....

....

....

....

....

....

....

....

....

....

Notes

....

....

....

....

....

....

....

....

....

....

....

....

....

Notes

....

....

....

....

....

....

....

....

....

....

....

....

....

Notes

....

....

....

....

....

....

....

....

....

....

....

....

....

Notes

....

....

....

....

....

....

....

....

....

....

....

....

....

....

Notes

Notes

....

....

....

....

....

....

....

....

....

....

....

....

....

Notes

....

....

....

....

....

....

....

....

....

....

....

....

....

Notes

Notes

....

....

....

....

....

....

....

....

....

....

....

....

....

Notes

....
....
....
....
....
....
....
....
....
....
....
....
....

Notes

....

....

....

....

....

....

....

....

....

....

....

....

....

....

Notes

....

....

....

....

....

....

....

....

....

....

....

....

....

Notes

....

....

....

....

....

....

....

....

....

....

....

....

....

Notes

....

....

....

....

....

....

....

....

....

....

....

....

....

Notes

Notes

....

....

....

....

....

....

....

....

....

....

....

....

....

Notes

....

....

....

....

....

....

....

....

....

....

....

....

....

Notes

....

....

....

....

....

....

....

....

....

....

....

....

....

Notes

Notes

Albion College
Alfred University
Allegheny College
American University
Amherst College
Arizona State University
Auburn University
Babson College
Ball State University
Bard College
Barnard College
Bates College
Baylor University
Beloit College
Bentley College
Binghamton University
Birmingham Southern College
Boston College
Boston University
Bowdoin College
Brandeis University
Brigham Young University
Brown University
Bryn Mawr College
Bucknell University
Cal Poly
Cal Poly Pomona
Cal State Northridge
Cal State Sacramento
Caltech
Carleton College
Carnegie Mellon University
Case Western Reserve
Centenary College of Louisiana
Centre College
Claremont McKenna College
Clark Atlanta University
Clark University
Clemson University
Colby College
Colgate University
College of Charleston
College of the Holy Cross
College of William & Mary
College of Wooster
Colorado College
Columbia University
Connecticut College
Cornell University
Creighton University
CUNY Hunters College
Dartmouth College
Davidson College
Denison University
DePauw University
Dickinson College
Drexel University
Duke University
Duquesne University
Earlham College
East Carolina University
Elon University
Emerson College
Emory University
FIT
Florida State University
Fordham University

Franklin & Marshall College
Furman University
Geneva College
George Washington University
Georgetown University
Georgia Tech
Gettysburg College
Gonzaga University
Goucher College
Grinnell College
Grove City College
Guilford College
Gustavus Adolphus College
Hamilton College
Hampshire College
Hampton University
Hanover College
Harvard University
Harvey Mudd College
Haverford College
Hofstra University
Hollins University
Howard University
Idaho State University
Illinois State University
Illinois Wesleyan University
Indiana University
Iowa State University
Ithaca College
IUPUI
James Madison University
Johns Hopkins University
Juniata College
Kansas State
Kent State University
Kenyon College
Lafayette College
LaRoche College
Lawrence University
Lehigh University
Lewis & Clark College
Louisiana State University
Loyola College in Maryland
Loyola Marymount University
Loyola University Chicago
Loyola University New Orleans
Macalester College
Marlboro College
Marquette University
McGill University
Miami University of Ohio
Michigan State University
Middle Tennessee State
Middlebury College
Millsaps College
MIT
Montana State University
Mount Holyoke College
Muhlenberg College
New York University
North Carolina State
Northeastern University
Northern Arizona University
Northern Illinois University
Northwestern University
Oberlin College
Occidental College

Ohio State University
Ohio University
Ohio Wesleyan University
Old Dominion University
Penn State University
Pepperdine University
Pitzer College
Pomona College
Princeton University
Providence College
Purdue University
Reed College
Rensselaer Polytechnic Institute
Rhode Island School of Design
Rhodes College
Rice University
Rochester Institute of Technology
Rollins College
Rutgers University
San Diego State University
Santa Clara University
Sarah Lawrence College
Scripps College
Seattle University
Seton Hall University
Simmons College
Skidmore College
Slippery Rock
Smith College
Southern Methodist University
Southwestern University
Spelman College
St. Joseph's University Philladelphia
St. John's University
St. Louis University
St. Olaf College
Stanford University
Stetson University
Stony Brook University
Susquhanna University
Swarthmore College
Syracuse University
Temple University
Tennessee State University
Texas A & M University
Texas Christian University
Towson University
Trinity College Connecticut
Trinity University Texas
Truman State
Tufts University
Tulane University
UC Berkeley
UC Davis
UC Irvine
UC Riverside
UC San Diego
UC Santa Barbara
UC Santa Cruz
UCLA
Union College
University at Albany
University at Buffalo
University of Alabama
University of Arizona
University of Central Florida
University of Chicago

University of Colorado
University of Connecticut
University of Delaware
University of Denver
University of Florida
University of Georgia
University of Illinois
University of Iowa
University of Kansas
University of Kentucky
University of Maine
University of Maryland
University of Massachusetts
University of Miami
University of Michigan
University of Minnesota
University of Mississippi
University of Missouri
University of Nebraska
University of New Hampshire
University of North Carolina
University of Notre Dame
University of Oklahoma
University of Oregon
University of Pennsylvania
University of Pittsburgh
University of Puget Sound
University of Rhode Island
University of Richmond
University of Rochester
University of San Diego
University of San Francisco
University of South Carolina
University of South Dakota
University of South Florida
University of Southern California
University of Tennessee
University of Texas
University of Utah
University of Vermont
University of Virginia
University of Washington
University of Wisconsin
UNLV
Ursinus College
Valparaiso University
Vanderbilt University
Vassar College
Villanova University
Virginia Tech
Wake Forest University
Warren Wilson College
Washington and Lee University
Washington University in St. Louis
Wellesley College
Wesleyan University
West Point
West Virginia University
Wheaton College IL
Wheaton College MA
Whitman College
Wilkes University
Williams College
Xavier University
Yale University

2794432

Made in the USA